JENNIFER TILLOCK, M.S. CCC–SLP

Unspoken Volumes

Writing Characters with Communication Challenges

First edition

ISBN: 979-8-9906153-0-4

This book was professionally typeset on Reedsy.
Find out more at reedsy.com

To the champions of unheard voices,

This book is dedicated to all who strive to amplify the stories waiting to be told. You who recognize the power of narrative to illuminate experiences often overlooked. You who understand the magic of creating characters who resonate, inspire, and challenge perspectives.

May Voices Unheard serve as a guide to crafting characters with communication disorders who are as real, relatable, and inspiring as the worlds you build.
With Gratitude,
Jennifer Tillock

Contents

Welcome to the World of Speech, Language, Hearing and Swallowing Disorders!

Have you ever wondered how to write a character with a stutter or a disability that affects their communication? This guide is your roadmap to creating authentic and inspiring portrayals of individuals navigating speech and language disorders.

Disclaimer

This book is intended for informational purposes only and is not a substitute for professional medical advice, diagnosis, or treatment. If you have any questions or concerns about a communication disorder, please consult a qualified Speech-Language Pathologist (SLP) or other medical professional.

1

Overview of Unspoken Volumes

Introduction: Weaving the Tapestry of Human Voices

I magine yourself nestled in a cozy café. Patrons chat in a lively hum of voices, each with its own unique rhythm and melody. A businessman barks orders on his phone, a group of friends shares laughter punctuated by regional slang, and an elderly couple whispers sweet nothings in a language you don't understand. This vibrant exchange showcases the remarkable tapestry of human communication.

But what happens when the threads of communication fray? As writers, we have the power to craft characters who navigate the complexities of language. To create authentic narratives, it's crucial to understand the spectrum of communication variations, disorders, and disabilities.

This book delves beyond the stereotypes often associated with communication challenges. We'll embark on a journey to explore the rich tapestry of human expression, from the subtle variations of accents to the intricate challenges of speech disorders.

Your Storytelling Toolkit:

This book equips you with the tools to navigate this sensitive topic with confidence. Here's what you'll gain:

- **Understanding Communication:** Explore the various types of communication variations, disorders, and disabilities, their impact on daily life, and how to portray them with sensitivity.
- **Crafting Inclusive Narratives:** Learn strategies to create characters who are not defined solely by their communication styles or challenges.
- **Character Development:** Delve deeper into the human experience through character questionnaires and empathy-building activities.
- **Collaboration and Resources:** Discover the importance of working with Speech-Language Pathologists (SLPs) and conducting research for accurate portrayals.

Moving Beyond Stereotypes:

Challenge yourself to go beyond the dramatic. Communication experiences encompass a vast spectrum, affecting individuals in unique ways. This book encourages you to explore the full tapestry, delving into lesser-known conditions and celebrating the resilience of those navigating communication challenges.

A Journey of Empathy and Empowerment:

By fostering empathy and understanding, we can shed light on communication challenges and dismantle stereotypes. This book empowers you to weave stories that celebrate the beauty and complexities of human connection in all its forms.

- **Ready to turn the page and embark on this exciting journey? Let's begin!**

2

Introduction to
Speech-Language-Hearing-Swallowing

Introduction: The Symphony of Communication - Exploring the Notes that Make Up Our Voices

I magine yourself nestled in a concert hall. The orchestra warms up, a symphony of instruments tuning their individual notes. As the conductor raises their baton, the instruments meld together, weaving a tapestry of sound that evokes joy, sorrow, and everything in between. Human communication is much like this intricate orchestra. Speech, language, hearing, and swallowing work in harmony to allow us to connect with the world.

But what happens when a single instrument goes out of tune? Speech-Language Hearing Sciences (SLHS) is the field dedicated to understanding, evaluating, and treating the disruptions that can occur within this magnificent symphony. From the melody of spoken words to the rhythm of swallowing, each element of SLHS plays a crucial role in how we express ourselves and interact with others.

This book delves into the four pillars of SLHS, exploring the fascinating intricacies of each. We'll journey through:

- **Speech:** The conductor, directing the flow of breath and articulation to create clear sounds. We'll explore how disorders like stuttering, voice problems, and articulation difficulties can disrupt this flow, and the impact they have on an individual's confidence and ability to communicate.
- **Language:** The lyrical essence, encompassing vocabulary, grammar, and the rules for forming meaning. We'll delve into the complexities of language disorders like aphasia and specific language impairment, and how they can affect understanding, expression, and social interaction.
- **Hearing:** The foundation of perception, allowing us to interpret the world around us. We'll explore conductive and sensorineural hearing loss, their causes and severity, and the social and cognitive challenges they can present.
- **Swallowing:** The silent conductor, a complex reflex ensuring food and liquids reach their destination safely. We'll examine dysphagia (swallowing difficulty) and its potential consequences for health and well-being.

Throughout this exploration, we'll meet the dedicated professionals who help individuals regain or improve their communication abilities – Speech-Language Pathologists (SLPs) and Audiologists.

But why is this important for writers?

Understanding the spectrum of communication disorders equips you to create characters who are rich and multifaceted. You'll learn to portray the challenges they face with sensitivity, while also celebrating their resilience and unique communication methods. The following chapters will delve deeper into each disorder, providing you with the knowledge to craft authentic and nuanced characters who resonate with your readers.

Please note:

The information presented in this book is intended to provide writers with a general understanding of communication disorders. It is not a replacement for a professional evaluation by a qualified Speech-Language Pathologist (SLP). If you suspect someone may have a communication disorder, please consult with an SLP for diagnosis and treatment recommendations.

Ready to embark on this exciting exploration of human communication? Let's turn the page and delve into the world of SLHS!

For more information:

- **American Speech-Language Hearing Association:** https://www.asha.org/public/
- **Centers for Disease Control and Prevention: Language Disorders:** https://www.cdc.gov/ncbddd/developmentaldisabilities/language-disorders.html
- **Centers for Disease Control and Prevention - Communication with People:** https://www.cdc.gov/ncbddd/disabilityandhealth/materials/factsheets/fs-communicating-with-people.html
- **National Institute on Deafness and Other Communication Disorders:** https://www.nidcd.nih.gov/
- **American Speech Language Hearing Association:** https://www.asha.org/public/speech/disorders/adultsandl/
- **Mayo Clinic:** https://www.mayoclinichealthsystem.org/hometown-health/speaking-of-health/help-is-available-for-speech-and-language-disorders
- **NIDCD Statistics:** https://www.nidcd.nih.gov/health/statistics/quick-statistics-voice-speech-language

General Communication Character Checklist

This checklist is designed to help you develop a character with unique communication needs or styles in a sensitive and authentic way.

Character Background:

- Specific Communication Need/Style: What is the reason for your character's communication differences (accent, dialect, fluency disorder, voice disorder, language disorder, hearing loss, balance disorder, swallowing/feeding difficulty, Sign Language user, AAC user)?
- Age of Onset (if applicable): When did the communication difference develop (childhood, adulthood)? Was there a triggering event?
- Severity: How severe is the communication difference? Does it mildly disrupt speech or significantly impact communication?
- Cause (if known): Is there a known cause for the communication difference (e.g., neurological condition, injury, developmental delay)?

Communication Characteristics:

- Speech: Consider aspects like fluency, volume, pitch, quality, and intelligibility (if applicable).
- Language: Consider vocabulary, grammar, comprehension, reading, writing, and social language skills (if applicable).
- Hearing: Consider degree of hearing loss and use of assistive devices (if applicable).
- Balance: Consider frequency of dizziness and impact on daily activities (if applicable).
- Swallowing/Feeding: Consider swallowing difficulty, oral motor skills, sensory issues, and nutritional needs (if applicable).
- Sign Language/AAC: Consider fluency, type of Sign Language or AAC system, and access methods (if applicable).

Communication Strategies:

- Self-Monitoring: Is your character aware of their communication differences? Do they try to control them or avoid certain situations?
- Coping Mechanisms: What strategies does your character use to manage their communication challenges? What do they do when communication fails?
- Alternative Communication: Does your character use alternative methods (writing, assistive devices, gestures, pictures) to supplement speech or Sign Language/AAC?
- Medical Treatment/Therapy (if applicable): Has your character received treatment (speech therapy, occupational therapy, hearing aids, etc.)? If so, how has it impacted them?

Emotional Impact:

- Frustration: Does your character experience frustration due to communication limitations?
- Isolation: Does the communication difference lead to social isolation or difficulty making friends?
- Confidence: How does the communication difference impact your character's self-confidence and ability to communicate effectively?
- Anxiety: Does your character experience anxiety in situations where they might struggle to communicate?
- What do they wish others knew about their disorder/difference?

Additional Considerations:

- Impact on Daily Life: How does the communication difference affect your character's education, work, or social interactions?
- Support System: Does your character have a supportive family, friends, or educators/colleagues who understand their needs?
- Character Development: How does the communication difference shape

your character's personality, coping mechanisms, and social interactions?

Narrative Choices:

- Sensory Details: How will you describe the world through your character's perspective (limited sounds, visual cues for balance, etc.)?
- Internal Monologue: Will you use internal monologue to explore your character's thoughts and anxieties about communication?
- Representation: Will you depict Sign Language use visually or describe AAC use? Consider consulting a sensitivity reader if including specific signs or AAC interactions.
- Balance: Have you balanced authenticity with the need for clear and engaging storytelling?

Character Development:

- Strengths and Struggles: How does your character's communication difference impact their daily life and interactions with others?
- Beyond Communication: What are your character's strengths and personality traits beyond their communication style?
- Avoid Stereotypes: Have you avoided relying solely on the communication difference to define your character?
- Choices: Have you given your character choices in treatment and coping strategies?

Remember:

- This checklist is a starting point; not all characters with communication differences will experience all of these aspects.
- Research the specific communication need/style to ensure an accurate portrayal.
- Consider including resources for readers who want to learn more.

· Focus on your character's unique voice, resilience, and communication methods.

3

Speech Sounds

Articulation and Phonological Processes

Definition and Characteristics

The way your characters speak can reveal a lot about them! Here's how to consider articulation (precise movements of the speech organs to produce sounds) and phonological processes (patterns of sounds) when crafting characters with speech disorders:

- **Speech Mechanics:** Articulation is all about how the tongue, lips, and other parts of the mouth move to make sounds. Imagine your character – do they have trouble forming certain letters like "R" or "S"? Perhaps they lisp slightly or have a slight nasal quality to their voice. These details can add a layer of realism to your character.
- **Sound Patterns:** Sometimes, people might have trouble pronouncing certain sounds in a predictable way. This is called a "phonological process." For example, a character might leave off the endings of words (saying "ca-'" instead of "cat") or swap sounds around ("dweedle" instead of "needle"). These patterns can be a subtle way to hint at a speech disorder without overwhelming readers.

Please note:

The information presented in this book is intended to provide writers with a general understanding of communication disorders. It is not a replacement for a professional evaluation by a qualified Speech-Language Pathologist (SLP). If you suspect someone may have a communication disorder, please consult with an SLP for diagnosis and treatment recommendations.

The Building Blocks of Speech: Vowels and Consonants

Human speech is a symphony of sounds, meticulously crafted by our vocal tract. Understanding how these sounds are formed, specifically by distinguishing between vowels and consonants, provides the essential foundation for appreciating the complexities of spoken language.

It's important to remember that the categories and examples provided here focus on **English sounds**. The fascinating world of languages boasts a vast array of phonemes, with many languages utilizing sounds not found in English. This knowledge becomes even more valuable when exploring speech sound disorders and the fascinating ways communication adapts in unique ways.

This section introduces the two main categories of speech sounds: vowels and consonants.

Vowels: Vowels are produced with a relatively open vocal tract, allowing air to flow freely while the vocal cords vibrate. Their unique qualities depend on the shape of the mouth and tongue position. Think of vowels as the sustained notes in our speech melody - "a," "e," "i," "o," "u" (and their variations like "ah," "ee," "oo").

Consonants: Consonants add articulation and definition to our speech. They can be produced with:

- **Vocal cord vibration:** These are **voiced consonants**, where the vocal cords vibrate along with the airflow obstruction. Examples include "b," "d," "g," "v," "z," and "l."
- **No vocal cord vibration:** These are **voiceless consonants**, where the airflow is obstructed without vocal cord vibration. Examples include "p," "t," "k," "f," "s," and "h."

Consonants can further be categorized based on two key aspects:

Manner of Articulation: This describes how the airflow is obstructed.

- **Stops:** Complete closure of the airflow (p, b, t, d, k, g)
- **Fricatives:** Air forced through a narrow opening creating friction (f, v, s, z, th, sh)
- **Affricates:** A combination of stop and fricative (ch, j) - "ch" is like a "t" followed by "sh", "j" is like a "d" followed by "zh"
- **Nasals:** Airflow escapes through the nose (m, n, ng)
- **Glides:** Short, transitional sounds (w, y)
- **Liquids:** Airflow directed around the sides of the tongue (l, r)

Place of Articulation: This describes where in the vocal tract the obstruction occurs.

- **Bilabial:** Lips together (p, b, m)
- **Labiodental:** Upper lip meets lower teeth (f, v)
- **Alveolar:** Tongue tip touches the gum ridge (t, d, s, z, l)
- **Interdental:** Tongue tip goes between the teeth (th)
- **Velar:** Back of the tongue touches the soft palate (k, g)
- **Glottal:** Vocal cords are involved (h)

By understanding these classifications, we gain a deeper appreciation for the intricate mechanisms behind speech production. This knowledge becomes even more valuable when exploring speech disorders and the fascinating ways communication can adapt.

Articulation Disorders

Age of Acquisition (Age at time of first signs)

Developmental articulation disorders are difficulties with speech sounds that occur as children are learning to talk. These disorders make it hard for children to say certain sounds correctly, which can affect how well they are understood by others.

Imagine a young character who struggles with "L" sounds, saying "wuv" instead of "love." This can be a source of frustration for the child, adding another dimension to their personality.

Acquired speech disorders are problems with speaking that develop later in life due to factors like injury, illness, or medical conditions. These disorders can make it difficult for someone to produce sounds or speak clearly, often affecting their ability to communicate effectively.

Perhaps an older character used to speak clearly but now has a stutter or slurred speech. This can be a part of their backstory or a challenge they face in your story.

Types of Articulation Disorders

Delayed Articulation Development: Characters experiencing delayed articulation development may speak in a manner that is younger than their chronological age. This can add complexity to characters, especially in coming-of-age stories or narratives involving characters with developmental differences.

- **Typical Development and Age Norms:** Understanding typical speech development and age norms can help authors create believable characters of different ages. Younger characters may have simpler speech patterns, while older characters may exhibit more mature speech skills.

- Search for **norms from a reliable** source such as the following: https://www.nslhd.health.nsw.gov.au/CYFH/services/Documents/Speech_Development_Chart.pdf

Phonological Processes: Phonological processes are patterns of speech errors that may or may not be commonly observed in the speech development of children. These errors involve simplifications or adjustments made by young children as they learn to produce speech sounds and organize them into words.

Phonological processes reflect the child's attempt to simplify the complex adult speech patterns they hear around them. Understanding phonological processes can help authors create authentic dialogue for child characters and add depth to their portrayal of speech development in fiction.

Norms: Some processes may be developmental and occur naturally in children as they learn to speak, others are considered atypical. Look for **phonological processes norms at a reputable site** such as this: https://www.wpspublish.com/types-of-phonological-processes. A few examples are:

- **Fronting:** Characters may substitute sounds produced at the back of the mouth with sounds produced at the front, generally velar sounds with alveolar sounds. A child might say "tat instead of cat", "dame" instead of "game"
- **Backing:** The opposite of fronting, backing involves substituting sounds produced at the front of the mouth with sounds produced at the back, generally alveolar sounds with velar sounds. A child might say "back" instead of "bat", "dad" instead of "gag"
- **Gliding:** Characters may substitute liquid sounds with glide sounds, affecting their speech clarity and adding distinctive qualities to their dialogue. A child might say "wock" instead of "rock" or "lock"
- **Final/Initial Consonant Deletion:** Omission of consonant sounds at the beginning or end of words can give characters a unique speech pattern and contribute to their characterization. A child might say "ba" or "at" instead of "bat"

- **Stopping:** Characters may replace fricative or affricate sounds with stop sounds, altering their speech production and adding complexity to their dialogue. A child might say "tat" instead of "sat", "pat" instead of "fat", "dem" instead of "them"
- **Syllable Deletion:** Omission of syllables within words can affect characters' speech rhythm and cadence, reflecting their linguistic style or background. A child might say "nana" instead of "banana", "ocpus" instead of "octopus"

Dysarthria: Dysarthria is a motor speech disorder (affecting the muscles involved in speech production) resulting from damage to the nervous system.

Characterized by slurred or unclear speech, changes in voice quality, and difficulties with articulation, dysarthria can manifest in various degrees of severity. Authors can portray characters with dysarthria with sensitivity, highlighting the challenges they face in navigating communication and social interactions.

Apraxia: Apraxia of speech is a neurological disorder (condition affecting the nervous system) characterized by difficulty planning and coordinating the precise movements necessary for speech production.

Characters with apraxia may struggle to produce sounds or sequences of sounds accurately, leading to inconsistent speech errors and frustration. Authors can depict the frustration and perseverance of characters with apraxia as they navigate the complexities of speech production and communication.

Structural Differences That May Cause Speech Disorders

- **Cleft Palate:** A cleft palate is an abnormal gap or opening of the palate (roof of the mouth), which can affect speech sound production and resonance. Characters with cleft palate may experience difficulties with articulation, resonance, and nasal airflow, impacting their speech intelligibility and social interactions. Authors can portray the challenges and resilience of characters living with cleft palate, highlighting their unique experiences and journeys.

- **Tongue Tie (ankyloglossia):** This is a condition where the lingual frenulum, a small fold of tissue under the tongue that connects it to the floor of the mouth, is unusually short or tight. This tightness can restrict the movement of the tongue, especially the tip. It should be noted that tongue tie is generally not a concern unless it disrupts feeding as an infant. Characters with tongue tie may experience difficulties with speech articulation, feeding, and oral hygiene (clearing of food from mouth). Authors can depict the impact of tongue tie on characters' speech development and self-esteem, exploring themes of identity and acceptance.
- **Trauma or Surgery:** Traumatic injuries or surgical procedures affecting the oral structures can result in temporary or permanent changes to speech sound production. Characters recovering from trauma or surgery may undergo physical and emotional challenges as they adapt to changes in their speech and communication abilities. Authors can explore themes of resilience, adaptation, and identity in characters navigating the aftermath of trauma or surgery.

Sensory/Perceptual Speech Disorders

- **Hearing Impairment:** Hearing loss, partial or complete, can impact speech development and monitoring, leading to difficulties with articulation, speech perception, and language acquisition.

It is important to remember that hearing loss is on a *scale from mild to functionally or even completely deaf*, and depending on the frequencies of the loss, children may have different speech patterns.

Look at a **"speech banana"** (a visual representation of the range of frequencies of speech sounds) such as the following: https://ohns.ucsf.edu/audiology/education/peds

Characters with hearing impairment may communicate using sign language, speech, an alternative communication device, or a combination of all, depending on their individual preferences and experiences.

Authors can portray the rich diversity of characters with hearing impairment, highlighting their unique communication styles and cultural backgrounds.

- **Auditory Processing Disorder:** Difficulty processing auditory information may manifest as challenges with speech perception and production. Characters with auditory processing disorder may struggle to understand spoken language, follow directions, or discriminate between speech sounds. Authors can depict the frustrations and triumphs of characters navigating auditory processing disorder, highlighting their strengths and resilience in overcoming communication barriers.

Causes of Articulation Disorders

In crafting authentic characters with articulation disorders, authors must consider the various factors that can contribute to the development of these speech difficulties.

Understanding the causes and contributing factors behind articulation disorders can add depth and complexity to character development and storytelling. Let's explore some key factors that may influence the onset of articulation disorders in fictional characters.

Developmental Factors

- **Childhood Development and Articulatory Acquisition:** Articulation disorders often emerge during childhood as children are learning to produce speech sounds. Factors such as delayed or atypical speech development, difficulties with motor coordination, or differences in oral-motor skills can contribute to the development of articulation disorders. Characters may struggle with articulating certain sounds or sequences of sounds as they navigate the complexities of speech production during early childhood development.

- **Role of Genetics and Family History:** Genetics and family history can play a significant role in the development of articulation disorders. Characters may inherit genetic predispositions or traits that affect their speech sound production, leading to similarities or patterns of speech difficulties within families. Authors can explore the interplay between genetic factors and environmental influences in shaping characters' speech development and articulatory abilities.

Environmental Factors

- **Influence of Language Exposure and Learning Environment:** The language exposure and learning environment provided to children can impact their speech development and articulatory skills. Characters raised in multilingual environments or with limited exposure to spoken language may experience delays or differences in speech sound acquisition. Authors can depict characters' diverse linguistic backgrounds and experiences, highlighting the influence of language exposure on their speech development.

Socioeconomic Factors and Access to Intervention Services:

Socioeconomic factors, such as access to healthcare and intervention services, can influence the course of articulation disorders. Characters from disadvantaged or under-served communities may face barriers to accessing speech therapy or other intervention services, leading to delays or challenges in addressing their speech difficulties.

Authors can explore themes of equity and social justice in depicting characters' experiences with articulation disorders and the resources available to support their speech development.

Neurological factors

Neurological causes of articulation disorders stem from abnormalities or damage to the nervous system, affecting the brain's ability to control the muscles involved in speech production. This can result from conditions such as stroke, traumatic brain injury, cerebral palsy, or neurodegenerative diseases like Parkinson's disease or multiple sclerosis.

When the brain's control over speech muscles is compromised, individuals may experience difficulties with articulating sounds accurately, leading to speech impairments. Treatment typically involves addressing underlying neurological conditions and may include speech therapy to improve speech clarity and communication abilities.

By considering the developmental, genetic, environmental, and socioeconomic factors that contribute to articulation disorders, authors can create nuanced and realistic portrayals of characters with speech difficulties. Incorporating these factors into character backgrounds and narratives can add depth and authenticity to storytelling, fostering greater empathy and understanding for individuals living with articulation disorders.

Implications of Articulation Disorders

- **Psychological and Social Implications:**Articulation disorders can have far-reaching implications on a character's psychological well-being and social interactions. Authors can deepen their characters' experiences by exploring the following aspects:
- **Variability in Speech Production:** Characters with articulation disorders may experience variability in their speech production, with some days or situations being more challenging than others. Authors can illustrate this variability by depicting characters navigating different speech contexts, such as casual conversations, public speaking events, or stressful situations.
- **Challenges in Different Contexts:** Characters with articulation disorders

may encounter challenges in various contexts, including social settings, academic environments, and professional settings. Authors can portray the difficulties characters face in effectively communicating their thoughts and ideas, as well as the impact on their confidence and social interactions.

- **Impact on Self-esteem and Identity:** Articulation disorders can impact a character's self-esteem and sense of identity. Characters may feel self-conscious or embarrassed about their speech difficulties, leading to feelings of inadequacy or social isolation. Authors can explore the internal struggles characters face as they grapple with their speech differences and strive to find acceptance and belonging.
- **Strategies for Coping and Building Resilience:** Characters with articulation disorders may employ various strategies to cope with their speech difficulties and build resilience. This can include practicing speech exercises, seeking support from friends and family, or participating in speech therapy sessions. Authors can highlight characters' resilience and determination as they navigate the challenges of living with articulation disorders and strive to overcome obstacles in their personal and social lives.

By exploring the psychological and social implications of articulation disorders, authors can create multidimensional characters with rich inner lives and complex relationships. Incorporating these themes into character development and narrative arcs can add depth and authenticity to storytelling, fostering empathy and understanding for individuals living with speech difficulties.

Assessment and Diagnosis of Articulation Disorders

Evaluation Process: Authors seeking to realistically portray characters with articulation disorders must understand the assessment and diagnosis process. This involves a comprehensive evaluation conducted by speech-language pathologists (SLPs) to determine the nature and severity of the speech difficulties. The evaluation typically includes a combination of standardized assessments, informal observations, and interviews with the individual and their caregivers.

Speech Assessment Tools and Techniques:

Speech-language pathologists utilize various assessment tools and techniques to evaluate articulation disorders.

- **Standardized tests** that assess speech sound production, such as the Goldman-Fristoe Test of Articulation or the Phonological Assessment of Child Speech. These produce scores that are compared to thousands of other children to determine where the child's speech falls.

Additionally, SLPs may use informal measures, such as speech samples or dynamic assessment, to gain a comprehensive understanding of the individual's speech abilities and challenges.

- **Speech samples** are a vital tool for assessing articulation skills. During an evaluation, a clinician might ask a child to repeat words, phrases, or short stories, or record a child speaking while playing or telling their own story.

By listening carefully to these samples, the clinician can identify any sounds the child struggles to produce or consistently replaces with other sounds. This analysis helps pinpoint specific articulation errors and allows the clinician to tailor therapy approaches to address those difficulties.

For example, if a child consistently substitutes "w" for "r," the speech sample would reveal this pattern, paving the way for targeted exercises to improve "r" production. It also provides a measure of intelligibility, or how easily a child can be understood by others.

- **Dynamic assessment** in articulation assessment involves evaluating an individual's ability to produce speech sounds with varying levels of support and feedback.

Unlike traditional assessments that simply measure speech sound accuracy, dynamic assessment involves providing cues, prompts, or modeling to determine the individual's potential for improvement.

Speech-language pathologists use dynamic assessment to understand the individual's learning processes, identify strategies that may facilitate speech sound production, and tailor intervention approaches to meet their specific needs

This approach allows for a more individualized and responsive assessment process, providing valuable insights into the individual's articulation abilities and potential for progress.

Collaboration with Speech-Language Pathologists: Authors can accurately depict the assessment and diagnosis process by illustrating the collaboration between characters and speech-language pathologists. This collaboration involves open communication, mutual respect, and shared decision-making to develop an individualized evaluation plan and treatment approach. Authors can portray the supportive and collaborative relationship between characters and SLPs as they work together to address the character's speech difficulties.

Differential Diagnosis-Distinguishing Articulation Disorders from Other Speech Disorders, accents or dialects:

Differential diagnosis is essential in accurately identifying articulation disorders and distinguishing them from other speech disorders. Authors can illustrate the thorough assessment process conducted by SLPs to differentiate articulation disorders from phonological disorders, motor speech disorders, or other speech difficulties. This may involve analyzing speech patterns, considering linguistic factors, and ruling out underlying medical or developmental conditions.

Consideration of Co-occurring Conditions (e.g., Phonological Disorders):

Articulation disorders may co-occur with other speech or language difficulties, such as phonological disorders. Authors can depict characters undergoing comprehensive assessments to identify co-occurring conditions and understand the interplay between different aspects of their speech and language abilities. This holistic approach to assessment allows SLPs to develop tailored treatment plans that address the character's unique communication needs.

By accurately portraying the assessment and diagnosis process of articulation disorders, authors can provide readers with insights into the complexities of speech evaluation and the importance of collaboration between individuals and speech-language professionals. Incorporating these themes into narratives can enhance character development and promote greater understanding of communication disorders within fictional contexts.

Treatment and Intervention

Speech Therapy Techniques:

Authors seeking to authentically portray characters undergoing treatment for articulation disorders can explore various speech therapy techniques. These may include:

Articulation Drill Exercises: Characters engage in repetitive practice of specific speech sounds to improve accuracy and clarity. As the patient progresses, they move from using sounds in isolation (by themselves), to syllables, then words, phrases, sentences, then finally structured (as part of aand unstructured conversation.

Cuing and prompting: The best cue or prompt will depend on the individual client's needs, learning style, and the specific sound being targeted. A skilled SLP will assess the client and choose a combination of cues and prompts that are most effective for promoting accurate sound production.

Visual Cues:

- **Pictures:** Show pictures of objects that begin with the target sound (e.g., picture of a cat for the /k/ sound).
- **Mirrors:** Help clients see their tongue and lip placement during sound production.
- **Diagrams:** Use diagrams of the mouth and tongue to illustrate the correct positioning for the target sound.
- **Tactile Cues:**
- **Light Touches:** Gently touch the jaw, lips, or tongue to guide the client towards the correct placement.
- **Hand Placement:** Place your hand on the client's chin or cheek to provide stability during sound production.

Auditory Cues:

- **Modeling:** Clearly pronounce the target sound in isolation, syllables, and words for the client to imitate.
- **Minimal Pairs:** Use pairs of words that differ by only one sound (e.g., "ship" and "sip") to highlight the target sound.
- **Verbal Prompts:** Give clear and concise instructions on how to position the mouth and tongue (e.g., "Tip of your tongue behind your teeth for /th/ sound").

Kinesthetic Cues:

- **Blowing Activities:** Use straws, pinwheels, or other blowing activities to help practice sounds that require air movement.
- **Tongue Placement Exercises:** Guide the client through exercises to strengthen and improve tongue control. It should be noted that these are to strengthen the tongue muscles and non-speech oral motor exercises have been shown to have little impact on speech.

Phonological Awareness Training:

Phonological awareness refers to the ability to identify and manipulate the sounds that make up spoken language. It's a foundational skill for developing strong reading and writing abilities.

Here are some key phonological awareness skills with brief definitions:

- **Rhyming:** The ability to recognize words that have the same ending sounds (e.g., cat, hat, sat).
- **Syllables:** The ability to identify and count the individual sound units (syllables) within a word (e.g., clap-clap for "water").
- **Onset and Rime: Onset:** The first sound(s) in a spoken word before the vowel (e.g., /b/ in "ball"). **Rime:** The part of the syllable that follows the

first vowel sound and includes any consonant sounds that follow (e.g., "all" in "ball"). This skill involves recognizing and manipulating these sound parts.

- **Blending Sounds:** The ability to combine individual sounds together to form a whole word (e.g., /d/, /o/, /g/ blended becomes "dog").
- **Segmenting Sounds:** The ability to break down a spoken word into its individual sounds (e.g., saying /s/, /i/, /p/ for "sip").
- **Minimal pairs** are words that differ by only one sound. This technique involves practicing minimal pairs that contain the target sound to help differentiate it from other sounds. For example, practicing "ship" and "sip" to target the /sh/ sound.
- **Auditory Bombardment:** This technique involves exposing the client to the target sound in various contexts (e.g., minimal pairs, corrected productions) to improve auditory discrimination and production accuracy.

Surgery

In the case of tongue ties, cleft palate, or other structural causes, surgery may be involved. Tongue ties usually are not an issue for speech if the child was able to nurse appropriately.

Augmentative and Alternative Communication (AAC)

Characters may utilize AAC devices or systems to supplement or replace verbal communication, providing alternative means of expression while they undergo treatment. This can include signs or Sign Language.

Multidisciplinary Approach:

Authors can depict characters benefiting from a multidisciplinary approach to treatment, involving collaboration between speech-language pathologists, educators, and other professionals. This collaborative effort ensures that the character receives comprehensive support across various aspects of their communication and academic development.

- **Collaboration with Educators and Other Professionals:** In portraying characters' treatment journeys, authors can highlight the importance of collaboration between speech-language pathologists, educators, and other professionals.

This collaboration involves sharing information, setting goals, and implementing strategies to support the character's speech and language development in academic and social settings.

- **Importance of Family Involvement and Support:** Family involvement and support play a crucial role in the success of treatment and intervention for articulation disorders.

Authors can illustrate the impact of familial support on characters' progress and emotional well-being, highlighting the role of parents and caregivers in practicing speech exercises, reinforcing therapy goals, and advocating for their child's needs.

By incorporating these treatment and intervention approaches into their narratives, authors can create authentic and relatable portrayals of characters navigating the challenges of living with articulation disorders.

Through thoughtful exploration of therapy techniques, collaboration with professionals, and support from family members, characters can embark on transformative journeys of growth and self-discovery, ultimately finding their voice and place in the world.

Myth Debunking

Crafting believable characters requires understanding the nuances of human communication. Speech sound disorders (SSDs), also known as articulation disorders, can add depth and complexity to your characters. However, these disorders are often shrouded in myths and stereotypes. Here's how to avoid perpetuating misconceptions when writing characters with SSDs.

- **Myth: Speech sound disorders equal low intelligence.**

This is simply untrue. Speech sound disorders are completely unrelated to a person's cognitive abilities. A character with an articulation disorder can be a brilliant scientist or a cunning villain. Don't relegate them to stereotypical roles based on their speech.

- **Myth: Only children have speech sound disorders.**

While speech sound disorders are more common in children, adults can experience them too. Explore the impact on a seasoned detective with a lisp or a world-weary warrior struggling with a stutter. Consider how their disorder might affect their interactions with authority figures or younger characters.

- **Myth: Everyone outgrows speech sound disorders.**

Early intervention is crucial for some children with SSDs. Consider the challenges faced by a character who never received therapy, impacting their social interactions and career. Perhaps they compensate by being a skilled writer or a talented artist, showcasing alternative strengths.

- **Myth: Speech sound disorders are caused by laziness or lack of effort.**

Speech sound disorders are not a choice. They can be caused by various factors beyond a person's control, such as tongue weakness, difficulty coordinating oral movements, or even hearing impairments. Show the character's frustration and their efforts to overcome these limitations, highlighting their determination.

- **Myth: People with speech sound disorders can't communicate effectively.**

This is a misconception. People with SSDs often use alternative words or expressions to convey their message. Give your character creative ways to express themselves, highlighting their resilience and resourcefulness. Perhaps they have a signature phrase that becomes their trademark, or maybe they rely heavily on body language to convey emotions.

- **Myth: Speech sound disorders predict learning difficulties.**

The two aren't always linked. Explore a character with an SSD who excels academically, defying expectations. Perhaps they have a photographic memory or a natural talent for math, showcasing their strengths despite communication challenges.

- **Myth: People with speech sound disorders should avoid public speaking.**

With proper therapy and practice, individuals can improve their speech clarity. Show a character overcoming their anxiety to deliver a powerful speech, proving that their voice deserves to be heard.

Remember:

By understanding and avoiding these myths, you can create characters with SSDs who are well-rounded and relatable. Let your characters speak their truth, free from stereotypes.

Portraying Characters with Articulation Disorders: A Guide for Authors

Authentic Representation:

When depicting characters with articulation disorders, authenticity is paramount. Authors should strive to capture the nuances of speech patterns and the lived experiences of individuals with these disorders. This involves conducting research, consulting with speech-language professionals, and listening to firsthand accounts from individuals with articulation disorders to ensure accurate and respectful portrayal.

- **Understanding the Complexity of Speech Patterns:** Articulation disorders manifest in a variety of ways, and characters may exhibit a range of speech errors and challenges. Authors should understand the complexity of speech patterns associated with articulation disorders, including distortions, substitutions, omissions, and additions. By accurately portraying these nuances, authors can create well-rounded and believable characters.
- **Balancing Realism with Narrative Flow:** While realism is important, authors must also balance it with narrative flow. Characters' speech difficulties should enhance the story rather than detract from it. This may involve finding a balance between accurately depicting speech errors and maintaining readability and coherence in dialogue. Authors can use techniques such as selective representation and contextual cues to convey characters' speech difficulties without overwhelming the narrative.

Sensitivity and Empathy:

Portraying characters with articulation disorders requires sensitivity and empathy. Authors should approach these portrayals with respect and compassion, recognizing the challenges individuals with these disorders face.

This may involve exploring characters' emotions, frustrations, and triumphs with depth and empathy, highlighting their resilience and humanity.

- **Avoiding Stereotypes and Caricatures:** It's essential to avoid falling into stereotypes or caricatures when depicting characters with articulation disorders. Characters should be multidimensional and avoid reducing them to their speech difficulties alone. Authors should strive to portray characters with articulation disorders as fully realized individuals with unique personalities, backgrounds, and aspirations.
- **Depicting Characters' Struggles and Triumphs with Respect:** Characters with articulation disorders navigate a range of struggles and triumphs in their daily lives. Authors can depict these experiences with respect and authenticity, acknowledging the challenges characters face while also celebrating their strengths and achievements. By portraying characters' struggles and triumphs with respect, authors can create compelling and empathetic narratives that resonate with readers.

In conclusion, portraying characters with articulation disorders requires careful consideration, research, and empathy. By striving for authentic representation, understanding the complexity of speech patterns, balancing realism with narrative flow, and approaching portrayals with sensitivity and respect, authors can create nuanced and impactful characters that enrich their stories and foster greater understanding and empathy.

Example Dialogues

Phonological Processes of fronting and gliding

The morning sun streamed through the kitchen window, painting golden stripes across the table where Maya, a spritely seven-year-old with pigtails the color of spun sunshine, sat hunched over her cereal. A frown creased her tiny forehead.

"Gwandpa," she called out, her voice dripping with concern, "is the

titty sick?"

Her grandfather, a weathered man with a shock of white hair, looked up from his newspaper. He peered over his glasses at the ginger cat, Marmalade, sprawled languidly on a sunbeam by the window.

"Why do you ask, Maya?" he inquired, his voice a gentle rumble.

"Betause," Maya declared, her voice dropping to a hushed whisper, "he's not doin' his pouncey thin'!"

Grandpa chuckled, a warm sound that filled the kitchen. "His pouncey thing?"

"Yeah!" Maya exclaimed, her frown deepening. "Evewy mohnin', he jumps on the tuhtains and they doh 'whoosh!' wite a bid wave."

Marmalade, as if on cue, twitched his tail and let out a languid yawn, barely lifting his head.

"Maybe Marmalade's just a little sleepy today," Grandpa suggested, reaching out to scratch the cat behind the ear.

Maya's eyes widened. "Sweepy? But it's mornin'! Sweepy time is for night-night, not for after bweatfast!"

Grandpa smiled. "Well, sometimes even kitties need to rest during the day, little one. Just like us."

Maya pondered this for a moment, her brow furrowed in concentration. Then, a grin spread across her face. "Otay, fine," she conceded. "But if he doesn't do his pouncey thin' soon, I'm doin' to have to dive him a bid hud to wate him up!"

Grandpa chuckled again, shaking his head fondly. "I'm sure Marmalade will be up and pouncing in no time, Maya. But maybe a cuddle wouldn't hurt either."

Dysarthria

Rain lashed against the diner window, blurring the neon lights outside. Inside, Ben huddled in a corner booth, his gaze fixed on the chipped mug of coffee in front of him. A waitress with a friendly smile approached him.

"*Hey there, hon. What can I getcha?*" *she chirped.*

Ben attempted a smile, the effort momentarily twisting his features. "*Uh... I'd like a... a... bweakfath burritto,*" *he mumbled, his words slurred together.*

The waitress leaned in slightly, her brow furrowed in concern. "*Breakfast burrito, you say? Sure thing, honey. Anything else to drink besides that coffee?*"

Ben winced slightly, his hand trembling as he held the mug. "*Jus... jutht the coffee,*" *he stammered, the "th" sound barely escaping his lips.*

The waitress nodded, her smile remaining kind. "*Alright, one breakfast burrito and a coffee coming right up. You alright there, buddy? You seem a little out of sorts.*"

Ben shook his head, the movement slow and deliberate. "*Jus' a... a bad night,*" *he mumbled, his voice thick and sluggish.*

The waitress patted his arm gently. "*Rough nights happen. Your coffee's on the house. You take care, alright?*"

Ben managed a weak nod, a wave of gratitude washing over him. As the waitress disappeared, he took a tentative sip of coffee. The heat stung his tongue momentarily, a jolt in the sluggishness of his body. He winced again as his hand trembled, nearly spilling the mug. Yet, he persevered, each small action a victory against the slurred speech and sluggish muscles that plagued him. He would finish his coffee, enjoy his breakfast burrito, and face the day, one blurry step at a time.

Here's how to handle portraying a character with chronic slurred speech after establishing their speech patterns:

Maintaining Clarity:

- **Focus on Meaning, Not Mechanics:** Once the reader understands the character's speech patterns, focus on conveying the meaning of their words rather than constantly describing the slurring.

- **Shift to Internal Dialogue:** For internal thoughts and feelings, you can switch to clear, un-slurred internal monologue for better clarity.

Adding Emphasis:

- **Return to Descriptions:** When the character's speech becomes particularly slurred due to emotional intensity, fatigue, or intoxication, reintroduce descriptions of slurring to emphasize the situation.
- **Non-verbal Cues:** Use non-verbal cues like facial contortions, hesitations, or tremors to highlight moments of difficulty when speaking. This can add depth and nuance without constant descriptions.

Balancing Description and Flow:

- **Readability:** Strike a balance between reminding the reader of the speech patterns and maintaining a natural reading flow. Too much description can become tedious.
- **Scene Importance:** If the character's speech becomes a crucial plot point requiring clear understanding, briefly describe the slurring to avoid confusion.

Example:

- **Scene established:** The reader knows Jake has slurred speech due to earlier descriptions.
- **Dialogue without constant description:** "The sun beat down on the dusty road," Jake muttered, wiping sweat from his brow. "Gonna be a scorcher."
- **Emphasis through non-verbal cues:** Frustration simmered in Jake's eyes. "I can't find it anywhere!" he stammered, his voice growing thick with each word.
- **Reintroducing descriptions for emphasis:** "Jus'... gotta get outta here," Jake mumbled, his words slurring badly. Fatigue pulled at him, making

his speech sluggish and imprecise.

By following these tips, you can maintain the character's distinct speech patterns while keeping your narrative engaging and clear.

Conclusion

Throughout this guide, we've explored the intricacies of articulation disorders and their impact on individuals, emphasizing the importance of authentic representation in literature.

We've delved into the complexities of these disorders, from developmental challenges to acquired conditions. Understanding these complexities allows authors to portray characters' struggles and triumphs with sensitivity and avoid stereotypes. By crafting compelling narratives that resonate with readers, we can foster empathy and understanding.

As writers, we have the power to celebrate the diversity of human experience by portraying characters with articulation disorders in a nuanced and human way. This approach challenges misconceptions and fosters empathy through storytelling.

Embracing diversity in our characters empowers readers to see the world through different perspectives. It allows us to celebrate a wider range of voices, including those of individuals with articulation disorders, and amplify their stories in literature.

Ultimately, our responsibility as authors extends beyond entertainment. We have the power to create a more inclusive and compassionate literary landscape by portraying characters with articulation disorders authentically and respectfully.

In conclusion, let us continue to champion authentic representation, challenge stereotypes, and amplify diverse voices. Through empathetic and genuine portrayals of articulation disorders, we can create stories that resonate deeply with readers and promote a more inclusive society.

For More Information:

· **Articulation and Phonology:** https://www.asha.org/practice-portal/clinical-topics/articulation-and-phonology/
· **Phonological Processes:** https://www.wpspublish.com/types-of-phonological-processes
· **Woman with verbal apraxia:** https://youtu.be/ngy8YTe1nHY?si=P7g8mIQMyRP1Z9cP
· **Adult Apraxia of Speech:** https://youtu.be/bZ7pnmd9UHI?si=BmNoLGAcsDVlwP4I
· **Phonological Disorder in Children: Common Patterns and Treatment:** https://youtu.be/4puWAd-ZztM?si=tcHij_cAO1yBn5LZ
· **Apraxia - The Mayo Clinic** https://www.mayoclinic.org/diseases-conditions/childhood-apraxia-of-speech/symptoms-causes/syc-20352045
· **Dysarthria - The Mayo Clinic** https://www.mayoclinic.org/diseases-conditions/dysarthria/diagnosis-treatment/drc-20371999
· **Apraxia Kids:** http://www.apraxia-kids.org
· **American Stroke Association:** https://www.stroke.org/en/
· **Motor Neuron Disease Association:** https://www.mndassociation.org/
· **An Aphasiologist Has a Stroke (Dysarthria):** https://youtu.be/LLhXxBC9xYk?si=x_-Qq3qlhCF3vcdd

Character Checklist: Speech Sound Disorders

This checklist is designed to help you develop a character with a speech sound disorder (SSD) in a sensitive and authentic way.

Character Background:

· Specific Speech Sound Disorder (SSD): What type of SSD does your character have? (e.g., Articulation Disorder, Phonological Disorder, Apraxia of Speech)

- Age of Onset: Did the SSD develop in childhood or later in life (e.g., due to stroke or brain injury)?
- Severity: How severe is the SSD? Does it mildly affect a few sounds, or significantly impact intelligibility?
- Cause (if known): Is there a known cause for the SSD (e.g., oral motor weakness, hearing loss)?
- How/when were they diagnosed? How did they feel about it? Did it change anything for them? Did they receive helpful advice/recommendations?

Speech Characteristics:

- Sound Substitutions: Does your character substitute certain sounds for others? (e.g., saying "wabbit" for "rabbit")
- Sound Omissions: Does your character omit certain sounds entirely? (e.g., saying "tou" for "town")
- Sound Distortions: Does your character distort certain sounds? (e.g., lisping)
- Speech Clarity: How understandable is your character's speech? Does it require extra effort from listeners?

Communication Strategies:

- Self-Monitoring: Is your character aware of their speech difficulties? Do they try to correct themselves? What are their primary coping strategies?
- Avoidance: Does your character avoid certain words or situations due to their speech difficulties?
- Augmentative and Assistive Communication (AAC): Does your character use any assistive technologies, such as communication apps or visual supports? Do they use non-tech modes such as Sign Language or writing?

Emotional Impact:

- Misunderstandings: How does your character react when others point out their disability? How do they react when others can't understand them?
- Frustration: Does your character experience frustration due to their communication challenges?
- Isolation: Does the SSD lead to social isolation or difficulty making friends?
- Confidence: How does the SSD impact your character's self-confidence and self-esteem?
- What does your character wish the world knew about their disability?

Additional Considerations:

- Treatment: Has your character received speech therapy or other treatment? If so, how has it impacted their speech? How did they feel about it?
- Support System: Does your character have a supportive family, friends, or teachers who help them manage their SSD?
- Character Development: How does the SSD shape your character's personality, goals, and relationships?

Narrative Choices:

- How have you incorporated the character's communication differences into the dialogue?
- Did you consider using internal monologue to explore the character's inner thoughts and anxieties?
- Have you balanced authenticity with the need for clear and engaging storytelling?

Character Development:

- How does the character's SSD impact their daily life and interactions with others?
- What are the character's strengths and how do they cope with the challenges of their SSD?
- Have you avoided relying solely on the SSD to define your character?
- Have you given your character treatment and coping options?

Representation:

- Did you use respectful and current terminology to describe the SSD?
- Did you portray the SSD realistically, avoiding stereotypes or exaggerations?
- Have you considered including assistive technologies the character might use?

Beyond the Disability:

- What are the character's dreams, goals, and passions?
- How can you showcase the character's unique personality beyond their SSD?
- Does your portrayal challenge assumptions about people with SSDs?

Remember:

- This checklist is a starting point; not every character with an SSD will experience all of these aspects.
- Research the specific type of SSD your character has to ensure accurate portrayal.
- Consider including resources for readers who want to learn more.
- Focus on the character's strengths and unique voice, not just their communication challenges.

Challenge Accepted? Speaking with an Articulation Disorder for a Day to Deepen Your Characters

Crafting characters with articulation disorders requires empathy and understanding. While research is crucial, there's no substitute for experiencing a communication challenge firsthand. So, here's a bold proposition: **try speaking with an articulation disorder for a day.**

Yes, you read that right. For 24 hours, consciously substitute certain sounds in your speech. For example, you could replace "k" sounds with "t" sounds ("bat" instead of "back") or "r" sounds with "w" sounds ("wow" instead of "road").

It won't perfectly replicate the complexities of an articulation disorder, but it can offer a glimpse into the frustrations and challenges faced by those who experience them daily. You will be changing your speech much like therapy works to change those with speech disorders.

Why Speak with an Articulation Disorder for a Day?

- **Empathy Through Experience:** This exercise isn't about mockery. It's about stepping outside your comfort zone to understand the emotional and even physical impact of an articulation disorder and trying to overcome it.
- **Beyond Stereotypes:** Articulation disorders often get reduced to a lisp in fiction. This challenge can help you create a more nuanced and realistic portrayal.
- **Respectful Representation:** By experiencing the frustration of mispronunciations, you gain a deeper respect for the resilience and communication strategies people with articulation disorders develop.

Important Considerations:

- **Sensitivity:** This challenge is meant to be a learning experience, not a mockery. Be mindful of the realities of articulation disorders and avoid perpetuating stereotypes.
- **Safety and Comfort:** If you have any pre-existing speech conditions, consult a doctor before attempting this exercise. Stop if you feel uncomfortable or frustrated.
- **Focus on Communication:** Remember, the goal is to understand the communication challenges, not to become a flawless impersonator.

The Power of Vulnerability

This challenge isn't about perfection. It's about opening yourself up to a new perspective. By experiencing the frustration of mispronunciations, even for a day, you can develop a deeper understanding of the characters you create. This empathy will translate into richer, more authentic portrayals, and ensure your characters with articulation disorders are not defined by their communication struggles, but by their strength and resilience.

Are you ready to accept the challenge?

4

Accents and Dialects

The Spice of Communication

L anguage is a living, breathing thing, constantly evolving and adapting. Accents and dialects are a beautiful testament to this evolution, reflecting the rich tapestry of cultures and backgrounds that shape how we speak.

Understanding the Nuances:

- **Accents vs. Dialects:** Both accents and dialects involve variations in speech, but with a key difference. Accents primarily focus on pronunciation, like the distinctive "r" dropped by some Boston speakers or the Southern drawl. Dialects, on the other hand, encompass a broader range of variations, including pronunciation, vocabulary (think "y'all" in the South or "wicked" in New England), and even grammar rules (like the verb usage in African American Vernacular English).
- **English Language Learners vs. Dialects:** It's important to distinguish between accents and dialects and the speech of English Language Learners (ELLs). ELLs are still acquiring English, so their speech may be influenced by their native language, leading to pronunciation differences,

vocabulary gaps, or grammatical errors. These are not mistakes, but natural aspects of the language learning process.

- **Articulation Disorders vs. Accents:** While accents and dialects are natural variations, articulation disorders involve difficulty producing speech sounds correctly. A character with a lisp who struggles to pronounce "s" sounds would have an articulation disorder, not an accent.

Please note:

The information presented in this book is intended to provide writers with a general understanding of communication disorders. It is not a replacement for a professional evaluation by a qualified Speech-Language Pathologist (SLP). If you suspect someone may have a communication disorder, please consult with an SLP for diagnosis and treatment recommendations.

Bringing Characters to Life:

Accents and dialects can breathe life into your characters, grounding them in specific regions or cultures. Here are some key characteristics to consider:

- **Pronunciation:** How do your characters pronounce certain sounds? Does a character from Chicago soften their vowels, or perhaps a character from England has a distinct "th" sound?
- **Vocabulary and Phrases:** Does your character use regional slang or unique expressions?
- **Grammar:** Does the character's dialect have specific grammatical quirks?

By understanding these distinctions and incorporating them thoughtfully, you can create characters whose speech patterns feel authentic and avoid insensitive stereotypes. Remember, accents and dialects are not deficits – they are vibrant markers of identity and cultural heritage.

Beyond "Howdy" and "Wicked": A Deep Dive into Speech Variations

Everyone has an accent and a dialect, even you! These natural variations in pronunciation, vocabulary, and grammar are like fingerprints – unique markers of our background and experiences. As writers, embracing these differences allows us to craft characters who feel authentic and grounded in their world.

A Spectrum of Speech:

Characters with accents or dialects can exhibit a fascinating range of speech patterns:

- **Pronunciation Deviations:** Does your Southern belle soften her vowels, or perhaps your New Yorker clips his words? Explore how characters pronounce vowels, consonants, and even sounds like "r."
- **Lexical Differences:** Spice up your dialogue with regional slang or unique expressions. A character from California might "hang ten" (surf), while someone from Scotland might say they're "feeling chuffed" (pleased).
- **Syntactic Variations:** Delve into the grammatical quirks of different dialects. For instance, African American Vernacular English might use a verb form like "They be playin'" instead of standard English.

More Than Just Words: The Impact of Accents and Dialects

These speech variations can add a layer of complexity to your narratives:

- **Misunderstandings and Humor:** When characters with different accents or dialects interact, communication hiccups can lead to confusion, ambiguity, or even humor. Use these moments to highlight the challenges and humor of cross-cultural communication.
- **Social Barriers and Empathy:** Accents and dialects can create social barriers, making it harder for characters to understand each other. Explore how characters navigate these challenges, fostering empathy and understanding in your readers.

Where Do Accents and Dialects Come From?

These variations in speech aren't random – they're shaped by several factors:

- **Environment:** Geographic location plays a big role. People raised in the same region often develop similar accents due to shared history, social interactions, and cultural influences. Additionally, cultural background shapes how individuals use language and pronunciation.
- **Language Acquisition:** As we learn language from those around us, we pick up their speech patterns. Phonological rules (sound patterns) and the language learning process also contribute to developing unique accents and dialects.
- **Social Identity:** We may adopt speech patterns associated with our social groups, like ethnicity, nationality, or even socioeconomic status. Accents and dialects can be badges of belonging, reflecting our connection to specific communities. Persons who opt to learn other accents or dialects may face opposition from their home community.
- **Psychology and Perception:** Language anxiety and self-consciousness can influence how we speak. Individuals may modify their speech

depending on the situation or their desired social identity.

The Power of Words: Exploring the Social and Psychological Impact

Accents and dialects have a profound effect on individuals and society:

- **Self-Esteem and Identity:** Attitudes towards accents and dialects can impact self-esteem and identity. Positive reinforcement of linguistic diversity can boost confidence, while stereotypes and discrimination can be damaging. Explore how your characters feel about their own speech patterns.
- **Stereotypes and Prejudice:** Accents and dialects are often targets of stereotypes and prejudice. Challenge these misconceptions in your narratives, promoting cultural understanding and acceptance.
- **Social Inclusion and Exclusion:** Speech variations can influence social interactions. Characters may face barriers to communication or acceptance based on their accent or dialect. Show how your characters navigate these challenges.
- **Relationships and Communication:** Accents and dialects can impact interpersonal relationships by affecting how well people understand each other. Explore the nuances of communication and how characters build connections despite speech variations.

Including English Language Learners (ELLs):

When portraying characters who are learning English as a second or additional language (ELLs), it's crucial to distinguish their speech patterns from accents and dialects. ELLs are still in the process of acquiring English, so their speech may be influenced by their native language in several ways:

- **Pronunciation Differences:** ELLs might struggle with certain English sounds or sound combinations that don't exist in their native language.

- **Vocabulary Gaps:** They may not yet know the full range of English vocabulary and might use synonyms or simpler words to express themselves.
- **Grammatical Errors:** As they learn the grammatical rules of English, ELLs might make mistakes with verb tenses, sentence structure, or word order.

Avoiding Stereotypes:

It's important to avoid portraying ELLs solely through the lens of their language challenges. They are individuals with rich backgrounds and experiences. Showcasing their resilience, determination, and the beauty of their multilingualism can add depth and authenticity to your characters.

By understanding the complexities of accents, dialects, and the speech patterns of ELLs, you gain the power to create rich and nuanced

Understanding Speech Variations: From Assessment to Intervention

Accents, dialects, and the experiences of English Language Learners (ELLs) all contribute to the rich tapestry of language. As writers, navigating these complexities can add depth and authenticity to your characters. Here's a breakdown to guide you:

Assessing Speech Patterns:

- **Methods of Evaluation:** Trained listeners, acoustic analysis, and sociolinguistic interviews can all be used to assess speech patterns. These methods can help you depict characters undergoing evaluation, revealing details about their linguistic background and communication style.
- **Diversity Matters:** Cultural and linguistic backgrounds significantly influence speech patterns. Remember, accents and dialects are not deficits, but vibrant markers of identity. Avoid assumptions about

characters based solely on their speech.

Identifying Communication Challenges:

While accents and dialects are natural variations, communication challenges can sometimes arise. This might involve difficulty being understood or speech patterns hindering effective communication. Explore characters facing these challenges and how they impact their interactions and relationships.

Addressing Communication Needs:

- **Accent Modification and Dialect Coaching:** These techniques help characters modify their speech patterns for specific goals. Show characters practicing speech drills, mimicking target pronunciations, and receiving feedback to improve their communication skills.
- **Language Therapy for Improved Communication:** Speech therapists can address communication difficulties related to accents and dialects by focusing on intelligibility, social communication skills, and overall communication effectiveness. Portray characters engaging in language therapy sessions, highlighting their journey of self-improvement and achieving their communication goals.

Intervention with Sensitivity:

Respect and cultural awareness are paramount. Therapists and educators should be sensitive to characters' cultural backgrounds and linguistic identities when implementing intervention strategies. Emphasize this aspect in your narratives, showcasing characters navigating cultural and linguistic diversity as they strive for improved communication.

Including ELL Characters:

- **Unique Speech Patterns:** When portraying ELLs, remember their speech is distinct from accents and dialects. ELLs are still acquiring English, so their speech might be influenced by their native language.
- **Avoiding Stereotypes:** Go beyond language challenges. ELL characters have rich backgrounds and experiences. Showcase their resilience, determination, and the beauty of multilingualism to create authentic and well-rounded characters.

By understanding these concepts, you can craft characters whose speech patterns feel genuine and enhance your narratives with the richness of linguistic diversity.

Myth Debunking

Crafting believable characters requires capturing the richness of human communication. Accents, dialects, and the challenges of English Language Learners (ELLs) all add depth and texture to your characters. However, these aspects are often misrepresented or overlooked. Here's how to avoid stereotypes and create characters who communicate authentically.

- **Myth: Accents and dialects signal lower intelligence.**

This is simply untrue. Accents and dialects are regional variations of a language, not indicators of intellectual ability. A character with a thick Southern drawl can be a brilliant scientist, and someone with a strong Scottish accent could be a cunning politician. Don't limit your characters' potential based on their speech patterns.

- **Myth: "Slower" dialects and accents indicate laziness or carelessness.**

Evidence has shown that "slower" dialects and accents are actually producing roughly the same number of sounds per second as "faster" dialects. That drawl simply introduces more vowels or even syllables. For example, "there" might be produced as "thay-er" and "floor" might be pronounced as "floo-wer."

- **Myth: Accents and dialects are interchangeable.**

Accents and dialects are distinct. Accents are typically variations in pronunciation, while dialects may involve differences in vocabulary, grammar, and even syntax. Research specific accents and dialects to portray them accurately. Perhaps your character speaks with a Boston Brahmin accent, or maybe they have a strong Geordie dialect.

- **Myth: Everyone with an accent or dialect wants to lose it.**

Many people cherish their accents and dialects as part of their cultural identity. Explore characters who take pride in their heritage and communication style. Perhaps a young immigrant character uses a mix of their native language and English, showcasing their ongoing journey of language acquisition.

- **Myth: ELLs are "bad" at speaking English.**

This is a misconception. ELLs are actively learning and mastering a new language. Consider the challenges faced by a character who struggles with complex grammar but excels at visual communication. Maybe they rely heavily on body language and gestures to convey their emotions.

- **Myth: ELLs should avoid speaking English in public.**

This discourages communication. While fluency can take time, ELLs deserve a voice. Show a character overcoming their anxiety to participate in a class discussion, proving that their voice matters.

· **Myth: ELLs only speak their native language.**

This isn't always true. Many ELLs are multilingual and can switch between languages depending on the situation. Explore a character who code-switches between English and their native language, highlighting their fluency in both.

Remember:

By understanding and avoiding these myths, you can create characters who communicate in diverse ways, enriching your story. Let your characters speak their truth, free from stereotypes. Their unique communication style is a window into their background and personality.

Breathe Life into Your Characters: Authentic Portrayals of Accents, Dialects, and Beyond

The magic of storytelling lies in its ability to transport readers to different worlds and connect them with characters who feel real. When it comes to characters with accents and dialects, this authenticity is especially crucial. Here's how to create characters who resonate with readers and celebrate the richness of human experience:

Why Representation Matters:

Imagine a bookshelf overflowing with stories, but only a single shelf dedicated to the vast array of accents and dialects spoken around the world. Accurate representation in literature and media is essential for breaking down these walls. By portraying characters with accents and dialects authentically, we achieve several goals:

· **Promoting Diversity:** A diverse literary landscape reflects the vibrant tapestry of our world. It allows readers to connect with characters who share their own backgrounds or open their eyes to new cultures and ways of speaking.

- **Fostering Empathy:** Stepping into someone else's shoes is a powerful tool for building empathy. When readers encounter characters with accents and dialects that might be unfamiliar, they gain a deeper understanding of the challenges and experiences these individuals face.
- **Challenging Stereotypes:** Accents and dialects are often used as shorthand in storytelling, perpetuating tired stereotypes. By showcasing the complexity and richness of these speech variations, we dismantle these misconceptions and celebrate individuality.

Crafting Authentic Voices:

Breathing life into characters with accents and dialects requires dedication and careful attention to detail. Here are some techniques to elevate your portrayals:

- **Research is Key:** Immerse yourself in the world of your characters. Consult with language experts, cultural consultants, or native speakers to understand the nuances of the specific accent or dialect.
- **Listen and Learn:** Authentic speech samples are invaluable resources. Listen to recordings, watch documentaries, or even travel to regions where the dialect is spoken. Pay attention to rhythm, pronunciation, and vocabulary choices.
- **Show, Don't Tell:** Instead of lengthy explanations, subtly weave linguistic cues into your dialogue. Use regional slang, idiomatic expressions, or specific word choices that reflect the character's background.
- **Cultural Context Matters:** Language doesn't exist in a vacuum. Consider the cultural background and context that shapes your character's speech patterns.

The Power of Storytelling:

Stories have the power to not only entertain but also to transform. By portraying characters with accents and dialects authentically, we can:

- **Challenge Stereotypes:** Move beyond the predictable tropes and showcase the richness and diversity of human experience.
- **Broaden Perspectives:** Expose readers to the beauty of different cultures and ways of speaking, fostering a more inclusive worldview.
- **Cultivate Empathy:** By delving into the struggles and triumphs of characters with diverse speech patterns, we encourage readers to connect with them on a deeper level, fostering empathy and understanding.

Remember, every character has a story to tell. By portraying them with authenticity and sensitivity, we create narratives that resonate with readers, celebrate human diversity, and leave a lasting impact.

Examples

Here are some ways to write an Indian accent in dialogue:

Phonetic Spelling (Use sparingly): Occasionally use slight phonetic spellings to emphasize specific sounds, but overuse can be distracting. Here's an example: "Lost, you say? No vurr-ees!" ("worries" pronounced as "vurr-ees").

Word Choice and Grammar: Indians learning English sometimes use slightly different vocabulary or make grammatical errors. Here are some examples:

- **Vocabulary:** "Beautiful lady" (common term of address)
- **Grammar:** "You seem to be hopelessly lost-ed" (past participle used incorrectly)
- **Sentence Structure:** "See, this is Jama Masjid," (simple sentence

structure)

- **Missing articles:** "You come, you see sights" (omission of "the")

Informal Speech: Indians often use informal speech patterns. Include slang terms, contractions, and enthusiastic exclamations. Here are some examples:

- **Slang:** "Adventcha!" (informal pronunciation of "adventure")
- **Contractions:** "You'll see the Red Fort in no time"
- **Exclamations:** "Excellent choice!" "No problem!"

Non-verbal Cues: Use descriptive language to show the character's gestures and facial expressions that might accompany an accent. Here's an example: "Raj chuckled, a warm sound that put Sarah at ease."

Combining these techniques:

"Losted, you say? No vurr-eez! I am Raj, best rickshaw driver in all Delhi! I take you there quick and cheap, no problem!" (Uses informal speech, omits "the", and slightly emphasizes "worries")

Remember, the key is to be subtle and avoid caricature. Let the dialogue flow naturally while incorporating these elements to suggest an Indian accent.

Southern United States dialect:

The midday sun beat down on the dusty Georgia road, shimmering off the chrome of a beat-up pickup truck. Sarah, a young woman fresh out of college, stood by the roadside, map clutched in her hand, a frown creasing her forehead.

Suddenly, the truck screeched to a halt beside her, kicking up a cloud of red dust. A weathered face with eyes as blue as a summer sky peered out from behind the driver's side window.

"Well, howdy there, little lady," drawled the man in a thick Southern

accent, his voice slow and easy. "You look a mite lost. Need a lift somewhere?"

Sarah, startled, nearly jumped out of her skin. "Oh, hello! Um, yes, actually. I'm looking for Honey Creek Farm, but I seem to be hopelessly turned around."

The man chuckled, a deep rumble that seemed to come from his belly. "Honey Creek Farm, huh? Well, bless your heart, that ain't far from here. Hop on in, I'll give you a ride."

Sarah hesitated for a moment, unsure about getting into a stranger's truck. But the heat was oppressive, and she didn't want to be stranded. With a deep breath, she climbed into the passenger seat.

"I'm Sarah, by the way," she offered, extending her hand.

The man grinned, his wrinkles deepening around his eyes. "Jebediah's the name, but most folks just call me Jeb. Now, where'd you say you were headin'?"

"Honey Creek Farm," Sarah repeated. "My aunt lives there."

Jebediah slapped the steering wheel with his calloused hand. "Well, now, that's a coincidence! Your aunt, that'd be Mildred, wouldn't it? Sweetest woman this side of the Mississippi."

Sarah's eyes widened. "You know her?"

"Know her? Why, honey, Mildred's practically kin! We go way back. 'Sides, everyone knows everyone around here."

As Jebediah navigated the winding backroads, he filled the silence with stories about Sarah's aunt, his voice warm and his words rich with Southern charm. Sarah, initially apprehensive, found herself relaxing, lulled by the rhythm of his speech and the gentle sway of the truck.

Finally, Jebediah pointed to a white farmhouse nestled among rolling green hills. "There you go, little lady. Honey Creek Farm in all its glory. Mildred'll be tickled pink to see you."

Sarah thanked Jebediah profusely, feeling a pang of sadness as she climbed out of the truck. "Thank you so much for the ride, Jebediah. It was lovely meeting you."

Jebediah tipped his hat with a wink. "Don't you mention it, honey.

Y'all come back and see us anytime. We Southerners always love havin'
visitors. "

Sarah watched as Jebediah drove away, a smile playing on her lips.
The unexpected encounter had not only gotten her to her destination
but also offered a glimpse into the warmth and hospitality of the South.

The southern dialect in this example was incorporated through several techniques:

- **Vocabulary:** Words and phrases like "howdy," "bless your heart," "a mite lost," "ain't far," "y'all," and "tickled pink" are characteristic of Southern speech.
- **Grammar:** Simple sentence structure ("Honey Creek Farm, huh?") and contractions ("don't you mention it") are used frequently.
- **Pronunciation:** While not explicitly written, the slow and easy drawl is implied through the overall rhythm of the dialogue.

Here are some things to be careful of when writing dialects:

- **Overuse:** Don't stuff the dialogue with too many Southernisms or it will sound forced and stereotypical.
- **Consistency:** Maintain the dialect consistently throughout the character's speech.
- **Clarity:** Don't sacrifice clarity for authenticity. Ensure the meaning of the dialogue remains clear even with the dialect present.
- **Respectful Portrayal:** Avoid turning the dialect into a joke or making fun of the speaker.

Here are some additional tips for writing a Southern dialect:

- **Research:** Listen to recordings of Southern accents or read works by Southern authors to get a feel for the rhythm and vocabulary.
- **Focus on Meaning:** Let the dialect enhance the character and the story,

not distract from it.

- **Read Aloud:** Read the dialogue aloud to ensure it sounds natural and flows smoothly.
- By following these tips, you can effectively incorporate a Southern dialect into your writing, adding depth and authenticity to your characters and their world.

Conclusion

We've embarked on a journey through the fascinating world of accents, dialects, and the unique speech patterns of English Language Learners (ELLs). We've explored the importance of accurate representation in literature and media, delving into techniques to craft characters whose voices resonate with authenticity.

But the true magic lies in what you, the author, do with this knowledge. Here's how embracing linguistic diversity can elevate your storytelling:

- **A World Beyond Monoculture:** Imagine a bookshelf overflowing with stories, each shelf bursting with the vibrant tapestry of human language. By incorporating accents and dialects, you break down the walls of monoculture, creating a literary landscape that reflects the richness of our world. Readers get to connect with characters who share their heritage or embark on journeys of discovery into new cultures and ways of speaking.
- **Empathy Through Shared Humanity:** Stories have the power to transport us into the hearts and minds of others. When we encounter characters with unfamiliar accents or dialects, we begin to see the world through their eyes. Their struggles, triumphs, and vulnerabilities become our own, fostering a deep sense of empathy and understanding.
- **Shattering Stereotypes with Authenticity:** Accents and dialects are often reduced to tired tropes in storytelling. Clichés and oversimplifications not only do these characters a disservice, but they also perpetuate harmful stereotypes. By portraying the complexities and richness of

speech variations, you can challenge these misconceptions and celebrate the individuality of your characters.

As you embark on your writing journey, remember these key takeaways:

- **Do Your Research:** Immerse yourself in the world of your characters. Consult with language experts, cultural consultants, or native speakers to understand the nuances of their speech patterns. Listen to recordings, watch documentaries, and absorb the rhythm, pronunciation, and vocabulary specific to their background.
- **Show, Don't Tell:** Subtly weave linguistic cues into your dialogue. Use regional slang, idiomatic expressions, or specific word choices that paint a vivid picture of your character's background. Let the language itself tell the story.
- **Embrace the Context:** Language doesn't exist in isolation. Consider the cultural and social context that shapes your character's speech patterns. How does their background influence their vocabulary choices, sentence structure, or even humor?

The written word has the power to transform. By portraying characters with accents and dialects with authenticity and empathy, you can:

- **Challenge Stereotypes:** Move beyond predictable tropes and showcase the richness and beauty of human experience in all its diverse forms.
- **Broaden Perspectives:** Open doors for readers to discover new cultures and ways of speaking, fostering a more inclusive worldview.
- **Cultivate Empathy:** By exploring the lives of characters with diverse speech patterns, you create bridges of understanding and connection, encouraging readers to see the world through a new lens.

Remember, every character has a story waiting to be told. Let's strive to tell these stories with authenticity and sensitivity. By creating narratives that celebrate the symphony of human language and expression, we contribute to a richer, more inclusive literary landscape that reflects the beauty of our world.

Here's to the power of storytelling, and the voices waiting to be heard!

For more information:

- ASHA: https://www.asha.org/practice-portal/professional-issues/accent-modification/
- https://www.asha.org/practice/multicultural/phono/
- **Office for Civil Rights:** https://www2.ed.gov/about/offices/list/oela/index.html
- https://guides.lib.virginia.edu/c.php?g=525451&p=3591731
- **National Association of English Learner Program Administrators: https://www.naelpa.org/**
- **Teachers of English to Speakers of Other Languages: https://www.tesol.org/**
- **Department of Education:** https://www2.ed.gov/datastory/el-characteristics/index.html

Character Checklist: Accents, Dialects, and English as a Second Language (ESL)

This checklist is designed to help you develop a character with unique speech patterns in a sensitive and authentic way.

Character Background:

- Origin: Where is your character from originally? (Country, region, specific city/town)
- Age of Arrival (if applicable): If your character is not a native speaker, at what age did they learn English? Who did they learn it from? Was it easy or hard for them?
- Length of Time Speaking English: How long has your character been

59

speaking English regularly?

- Exposure to English: How was your character exposed to English? (Formal education, immersion, media consumption)

Speech Characteristics:

- Accent: Does your character have a regional accent? (e.g., British, Southern American)
- Dialect: Does your character speak a specific dialect? (e.g., African American Vernacular English, Scottish Gaelic)
- ESL Fluency: How fluent is your character in English? (Beginner, intermediate, advanced)
- Grammar and Vocabulary: Does your character make any grammatical errors or use vocabulary specific to their native language or dialect?

Communication Strategies:

- Self-Monitoring: Is your character aware of their accent or speech differences? Do they try to modify their speech?
- Code-Switching: Does your character switch between English and their native language/accent/dialect depending on the situation?
- Filler Words: Does your character use filler words or phrases ("um," "like") more frequently due to language processing challenges?
- Does your character avoid speaking due to their differences or difficulty being misunderstood?

Emotional Impact:

- Misunderstandings: How does your character react when others don't understand them due to their accent or language barrier?
- Frustration: Does your character experience frustration due to language barriers or limitations?
- Isolation: Does your character's language difference lead to social

isolation or difficulty making friends?

- Confidence: How does your character's speech pattern impact their self-confidence and communication skills?

Additional Considerations:

- Motivation for Learning English: Why did your character learn English? (Education, work, personal relationships)
- Learning Resources: How did your character learn English? (Formal classes, self-study, immersion)
- Cultural Identity: How does your character's accent or language background connect to their cultural identity?

Narrative Choices:

- Dialogue: How will you represent your character's accent or dialect in writing (spelling variations, phonetic sounds)?
- Internal Monologue: Will you use internal monologue to explore your character's thoughts in their native language or accented English?
- Balance: Have you balanced authenticity with the need for clear and engaging storytelling?

Character Development:

- Strengths and Struggles: How does your character's communication style impact their daily life and interactions with others?
- Beyond Speech: What are your character's strengths and personality traits beyond their accent or language background?
- Avoid Stereotypes: Have you avoided relying solely on their accent/ESL status to define your character?
- Choices: Have you given your character choices in how to cope?

Representation:

- Respectful Portrayal: Have you portrayed your character's accent or language background with respect and sensitivity?
- Avoidance of Caricatures: Have you avoided stereotypical or exaggerated representations of accents or ESL speakers?

Remember:

- This checklist is a starting point; not all characters with accents or language differences will experience all of these aspects.
- Research the specific region or language background to ensure an authentic portrayal.
- Consider including resources for readers who want to learn more.
- Focus on your character's unique voice and personality, not just their way of speaking.

Challenge Accepted? Speaking Pig Latin for a Day to Deepen Your Characters

Crafting characters who speak with accents, dialects, or who are English Language Learners (ELL) requires empathy and understanding. Research is crucial, but there's no substitute for experiencing a communication difference firsthand. So, here's a bold proposition: **try speaking in Pig Latin for a day**!

Yes, you read that right. For 24 hours, consciously translate your everyday speech into Pig Latin. Remember, Pig Latin involves moving the first consonant sound (or consonant cluster) to the end of the word and adding "-ay." For example, "hello" becomes "ello-hay" and "computer" becomes "omputer-cay."

It won't perfectly replicate the complexities of language differences or the challenges faced by ELL populations, but it can offer a glimpse into the potential frustrations and adjustments needed when communication doesn't flow as easily.

Why Speak Pig Latin for a Day?

- **Empathy Through Experience:** This exercise isn't about mocking accents or dialects. It's about stepping outside your comfort zone to understand the challenges of communicating in a different way. You might experience frustration or feel misunderstood, offering valuable insight into the emotional impact of language differences.
- **Beyond Stereotypes:** Accents, dialects, and the struggles of ELL characters often get reduced to quirky traits in fiction. This challenge can help you create more nuanced and realistic portrayals. Imagine the difficulty of ordering coffee or giving a presentation when you're constantly translating words in your head.

Respectful Representation: By experiencing the awkwardness of communicating in a non-native language or with a different pronunciation pattern, you gain a deeper respect for the resilience and communication strategies people with these backgrounds develop.

Important Considerations:

- **Sensitivity:** This is a learning experience, not a mockery. Be mindful of the realities of language differences, avoid perpetuating stereotypes, and respect others' communication styles.
- **Focus on Communication:** Remember, the goal is to experience the challenges of communicating differently, not to become a Pig Latin expert. Don't get bogged down in translating every single word perfectly.
- **Safety and Comfort:** This challenge is for fun and learning. If you have any pre-existing speech impediments, consult a doctor before attempting it. Stop if you feel overwhelmed or frustrated.

The Power of Vulnerability

This challenge isn't about perfection. It's about opening yourself up to a new perspective. By experiencing the communication hurdles that come with using Pig Latin, even for a day, you can develop a deeper understanding of the characters you create. This empathy will translate into richer, more authentic portrayals, ensuring your characters with language differences are not defined by their communication style, but by their strength, resilience, and the stories they have to tell.

Are you ready to oink-cept the challenge?

5

Fluency Disorders

Beyond the Stutter

Fluency disorders disrupt the smooth flow of speech, making communication challenging. These can be developmental, arising in childhood, or acquired later in life due to brain injury or illness. By understanding the different types of fluency disorders, we can dismantle stereotypes and promote inclusivity for individuals who communicate differently.

A Spectrum of Speech Disruptions:

Fluency disorders encompass a range of speech difficulties, not just stuttering. They can manifest as repeating sounds or syllables, prolonging sounds, having silent frozen periods, or jumbled speech.

These disruptions can be frustrating and lead to anxiety or social withdrawal for those affected. It's important to remember that fluency disorders, particularly stuttering, may be lifelong companions, not challenges to be "overcome." Let's celebrate neurodiversity and embrace communication differences.

Types of Fluency Disorders:

- **Developmental Fluency Disorders:** These emerge in childhood and may persist into adulthood. Stuttering is the most common example.
- **Stuttering/Stammering:** This well-known disorder disrupts the natural flow of speech, causing repetitions, prolongations, or blocks. Stuttering can vary in severity and may involve physical tension or avoidance behaviors like avoiding certain words or situations.
- **Acquired (Neurogenic) Fluency Disorders:** These arise from brain injury or illness, affecting speech production. They can occur at any age due to conditions like stroke, brain injury, or neurological diseases.
- **Cluttering:** This less common disorder involves rapid, disorganized speech that can be difficult to understand. Individuals who clutter may speak quickly with frequent interruptions and jumbled thoughts, making it challenging to organize their ideas clearly. Cluttering can sometimes co-occur with other speech and language difficulties.

Understanding these different types of fluency disorders allows authors to create characters with authentic communication styles and portray the challenges and triumphs they face. By dismantling stereotypes and fostering empathy, we can create a more inclusive world where everyone feels comfortable using their voice.

Please note:

The information presented in this book is intended to provide writers with a general understanding of communication disorders. It is not a replacement for a professional evaluation by a qualified Speech-Language Pathologist (SLP). If you suspect someone may have a communication disorder, please consult with an SLP for diagnosis and treatment recommendations.

Unveiling the Causes of Fluency Disorders: A Look Beyond the Stutter

Fluency disorders can significantly impact a person's ability to communicate effectively. While the exact causes remain under investigation, several factors are believed to contribute to their development. Here's a breakdown to guide you as you craft characters with fluency disorders:

Imagine the complex dance of muscles and nerves that allows us to speak. Fluency disorders often stem from disruptions in this intricate process, making speech production a challenge. This can manifest as repetitions, prolonged sounds, or involuntary pauses that disrupt the natural flow of communication.

The Role of Genetics and Family History:

- **Genetic Predisposition:** Research suggests that certain genetic factors may increase a person's susceptibility to developing fluency disorders. Here's an analogy to understand it better: Imagine a fire. Three elements are crucial for a fire to start: heat source, fuel, and oxygen. In this analogy, the **genetic predisposition** acts like the **heat source**. It increases the risk of a fire (developing a fluency disorder), but it's not enough on its own.
- **Family Connections:** Individuals with a family history of stuttering or other fluency disorders are more likely to develop similar speech difficulties. This suggests a potential genetic link, but environmental factors may also be at play.

Environmental Influences:

- **Early Language Exposure:** Children raised in multilingual environments or with a history of emotional stress may be more susceptible to speech difficulties. This doesn't mean these factors cause fluency disorders, but they can create situations where fluency might be challenged. If a child already has a predisposition for stuttering, having a more complex environment may cause its emergence, similar to how the presence of fuel (environmental factors) can influence a fire caused by a heat source (genetic predisposition).

- **The Learning Environment:** Educational practices and social interactions significantly impact speech development. Supportive learning environments can foster fluency, while chaotic or stressful situations might contribute to speech difficulties.

Socioeconomic Considerations:

Unfortunately, access to healthcare and speech therapy can be a hurdle for some families. Without proper diagnosis and intervention, fluency disorders can become more severe and long-lasting. This highlights the importance of creating accessible healthcare systems and promoting early intervention programs to ensure all individuals with fluency disorders have the opportunity to develop effective communication skills.

By understanding these potential causes, you can create characters with fluency disorders that feel authentic and believable. Remember, fluency disorders are not a reflection of intelligence and can be effectively managed with therapy and support.

Remember:

The exact causes of fluency disorders are complex and likely involve a combination of factors. Genetics, family history, environmental influences, and even access to healthcare all play a part. By understanding these complexities, you can create characters whose fluency disorders feel authentic and true to life.

Types of Fluency Disorders

Fluency disorders disrupt the smooth flow of speech, creating a unique communication style. These variations manifest in distinct ways, offering a glimpse into the lived experience of individuals who navigate speech differently. Here's a breakdown to guide you as you craft characters with fluency disorders:

Stuttering:

Stuttering is a common fluency disorder characterized by:

- **Repetitions:** Imagine someone saying "b-b-ball" instead of "ball." These repetitions can be sounds ("c-c-cat"), syllables ("ma-ma-man"), or even whole words ("go-go-go"). They can occur at the beginning, middle, or end of words, creating a noticeable break in the flow of speech.
- **Prolongations:** Ever heard someone say "sssnake" instead of "snake"? The speaker stretches or prolongs certain sounds, disrupting the natural rhythm of speech.
- **Blocks:** These are involuntary pauses or silent moments where the person struggles to produce sounds or words. Imagine a beat of silence filled with visible tension as the individual attempts to speak. These blocks can be silent or accompanied by physical effort, like lip movements or tensing of facial muscles.
- **Fillers:** We all use fillers like "um" or "uh" occasionally. For people who stutter, these fillers serve as placeholders or buffers, helping them navigate through moments of disfluency. They might use a wider variety of fillers, or use them more frequently, compared to someone with typical speech patterns.
- **Secondary Behaviors:** The struggle to speak fluently can lead to "secondary behaviors" like eye blinking, facial tensing, or even throat clearing. Imagine rapid blinking, a furrowed brow, or a quick cough. These are coping mechanisms individuals develop to manage their

stuttering, and their presence can vary depending on the severity of the stutter and the situation. Sometimes the secondary characteristics become more noticeable than the stutter itself.

Cluttering: A Rapid Rush of Words

Cluttering is another fluency disorder characterized by rapid and disorganized speech:

- **Disorganized Speech:** Imagine words pushed together or sounds left out, making speech sound rushed and jumbled. Listeners might struggle to follow the flow of the conversation as the speaker seems to be racing through their thoughts. Sentences might be grammatically incomplete, or words might be substituted with similar-sounding ones.
- **Fast Speech Rate:** The rapid pace of speech further contributes to the disorganization. The sheer speed makes it difficult for the speaker to maintain clarity and for the listener to understand the full message. Imagine someone talking so quickly that their words begin to run together, making it sound mumbled or breathless.
- **Fillers:** Just like with stuttering, people who clutter may use fillers like "um" or "uh" more frequently to compensate for the disruptions caused by the rapid and disorganized speech. They might also use phrases like "you know" or "like" more often as they try to bridge gaps or re-organize their thoughts mid-sentence.
- May not be aware of their cluttered speech.

By understanding these intricate details, you can craft characters with fluency disorders who feel genuine and relatable. Explore the unique ways they communicate, the challenges they navigate, and the strategies they develop to express themselves effectively. Remember, fluency disorders are just one aspect of a person's identity. There's a whole world waiting to be explored beyond the stutter or the rapid speech.

The Unpredictable Journey: Living with a Fluency Disorder

Fluency disorders don't present a constant challenge. For individuals who stutter or clutter, speech can be a landscape of shifting terrain. Periods of smooth communication can be punctuated by sudden stumbles, making it difficult to predict or control speaking difficulties. This unpredictability adds another layer of complexity to managing these disorders.

The Pressure to Perform:

Imagine the pressure to speak flawlessly in a job interview or a classroom presentation. For those with fluency disorders, these situations can exacerbate speech difficulties. The very act of trying to speak "perfectly" can lead to frustration and a sense of isolation.

Everyday Challenges:

Fluency disorders can cast a long shadow across various aspects of life:

- **Social Settings:** Fear of judgment or embarrassment can lead to social withdrawal. Individuals might avoid conversations or shy away from social gatherings to minimize the chance of struggles with speaking.
- **School:** Active participation in class discussions or delivering presentations can become daunting tasks. This can hinder academic performance and make connecting with classmates more difficult..
- **Phone Calls:** Simple phone conversations can transform into stressful experiences. The inability to predict or control disfluencies can lead to anxiety about being misunderstood or judged over the phone. Individuals with fluency disorders might avoid phone calls altogether, opting for text messages or email whenever possible, which can limit communication opportunities in both personal and professional settings.
- **Job Interviews:** The pressure to perform well in a job interview can

exacerbate fluency difficulties. The fear of disfluencies overshadowing qualifications and skills can create a significant barrier to employment opportunities.

- **Romantic Relationships:** Fluency disorders can impact dating and romantic relationships. The fear of negative reactions during conversations can lead to hesitation in expressing feelings or building intimacy. Open communication is essential in any relationship, and fluency disorders can create challenges in achieving that level of communication comfort.

Beyond Speech:

The impact of fluency disorders extends far beyond the spoken word. They can touch upon various aspects of a person's well-being:

- **Work:** Jobs that require a lot of talking, like sales or presentations, can become a source of anxiety. Individuals might struggle to find suitable employment opportunities or feel limited in their career choices.
- **Emotions:** Constant battles with fluency can chip away at self-esteem and confidence. Individuals with fluency disorders might feel frustrated, embarrassed, or inadequate due to their speech difficulties. This can affect their overall confidence and sense of self-worth.This can lead to feelings of isolation, social stigma, and a diminished quality of life.

Building Resilience:

Living with a fluency disorder requires strength and the ability to adapt. Several strategies can be instrumental in navigating these challenges:

- **Coping with Anxiety:** Mindfulness exercises and relaxation techniques can help manage anxiety associated with speaking situations.
- **Communication Skills:** Learning strategies to improve fluency, such as speaking slowly and deliberately, can empower individuals to express

themselves more effectively.

- **Building a Support Network:** Surrounding oneself with supportive friends, family, and professionals can provide a crucial source of encouragement and understanding.

By understanding the unpredictable nature of fluency disorders and their impact on an individual's life, you can create characters who are well-rounded and relatable. Explore the challenges they face, the strategies they develop, and the resilience they demonstrate as they navigate the world of communication.

Remember, fluency disorders are just one facet of a person's identity. There's a whole story waiting to be told beyond the stutter or the rapid speech.

Cultural Variations in Tolerance for Disfluency

While broad cultural trends exist, it's important to remember these are just that - trends. Individual experiences and attitudes within a culture can vary greatly.

Cultural values like power distance and collectivism can influence how stuttering affects people's lives (according to the source cited below).

Power distance refers to how comfortable a society is with unequal power structures. In societies with high power distance, people might be less likely to challenge authority figures who stutter, potentially leading to less social support.

Conversely, societies with low power distance might encourage open communication about stuttering, leading to more resources and understanding.

Collectivism focuses on group priorities. In cultures with high collectivism, people might be more likely to hide their stuttering to avoid disrupting social harmony.

In contrast, low collectivism cultures might be more accepting of individual differences, potentially leading to less stigma for those who stutter.

These cultural factors likely influence societal attitudes towards stuttering, which in turn can impact the daily experiences of people who stutter.

Yan Ma, Emmalee M. Mason, Evynn M. McGinn, Jordan Parker, Judith D. Oxley, Kenneth O. St. Louis, Attitudes toward stuttering of college students in the USA and China: A cross-cultural comparison using the POSHA-S, Journal of Fluency Disorders, Volume 79, 2024,106037, ISSN 0094-730X, https://doi.org/10.1016/j.jfludis.2024.106037. (https://www.sciencedirect.com/science/article/pii/S0094730X24000019)

It's All Relative:

Imagine two individuals with disfluency, one from Japan and one from the United States, applying for the same job in a multinational company.

● The Japanese applicant might find the interview environment more comfortable due to the cultural acceptance of pauses and hesitations.

● The American applicant might feel pressured to speak quickly and flawlessly, potentially exacerbating their disfluency.

Additional Considerations:

- **Age:** Children in most cultures are generally more tolerant of disfluency from their peers. As children develop and enter social situations with higher communication expectations, tolerance might decrease. Adults are also more tolerant of disfluency in children than adults.
- **Context:** A formal presentation might have a lower tolerance for disfluency compared to a casual conversation with friends.

Remember:

Cultural tolerance doesn't erase the challenges of disfluency. Individuals with disfluency can benefit from speech-language therapy and strategies to manage their communication difficulties regardless of the cultural context.

Unveiling the Puzzle: Assessing Fluency Disorders

Diagnosing a fluency disorder isn't a one-size-fits-all approach. It's a detective story, with speech-language pathologists (SLPs) piecing together clues to create a personalized treatment plan. Here's a breakdown to guide you as you depict this process authentically in your writing:

The Speech Assessment Toolbox:

Imagine a toolbox filled with specialized instruments. Assessing fluency disorders follows a similar principle. SLPs use a variety of tools to gain a comprehensive understanding of the individual's communication challenges:

- **Case History:** This detailed background delves into the person's speech development, communication patterns, and any relevant medical history. Think of it as the foundation, providing crucial context for interpreting the other assessment pieces.
- **Standardized Tests:** These pre-designed tests measure fluency using scoring systems. They might involve reading passages aloud or repeating sentences. Imagine a clinician using a specific test to quantify the frequency and type of disfluencies (repetitions, prolongations, blocks) present.
- **Speech Samples:** Clinicians record natural conversation or ask individuals to read specific texts. Analyzing these samples allows them to identify patterns of disfluency and their frequency. This is like taking a snapshot of the person's speech in action.
- **Observational Assessments:** Just as a detective observes a crime scene,

SLPs observe how a person speaks in different situations (one-on-one conversation vs. public speaking). This reveals how factors like anxiety or specific environments can influence fluency. Imagine observing how a character's speech becomes more disfluent during a presentation compared to a casual chat with a friend.

· **Self-reporting:** An individuals' rating of their own stuttering severity and experience can be a valuable tool in assessing fluency disorders. While not a substitute for clinical evaluation, it provides crucial insights into a person's experience and allows for evaluation beyond the clinical setting.

Looking Beyond the Stutter:

Fluency disorders sometimes come with "unwanted guests" – co-occurring conditions that can influence speech and language development. Here are a couple of examples:

· **Phonological Disorders:** These disorders affect how sounds are produced (e.g., difficulty pronouncing "r" or "l"). Someone who stutters might also have trouble with certain sounds, making their speech even harder to understand. Imagine a character who stutters and also has difficulty pronouncing their "r"s, making words like "friend" sound more like "fwiend."

· **Language Processing Disorders:** These disorders affect how the brain processes language. Someone with a fluency disorder might also struggle with grammar, vocabulary, or understanding complex sentences. Consider a character who stutters and also has difficulty formulating complete sentences, making their communication even more challenging.

· **ADHD:** Children with ADHD are more likely to exhibit speech disfluencies compared to their peers. While not all disfluencies indicate a fluency disorder, it's important to consider ADHD as a possible co-occurring condition during assessment to ensure appropriate diagnosis and treatment plans.

By considering co-existing conditions, SLPs can create a well-rounded treatment plan that addresses all aspects of a person's speech and language needs.

Adding Depth to Your Story:

You can incorporate these assessment methods into your narrative. Show a character taking a standardized test, feeling anxious in a public speaking situation where their fluency is challenged, or having a conversation with a speech therapist who explains the assessment process. Consider including a character who has a co-occurring condition. How does it affect their speech and communication alongside their fluency disorder?

Remember, fluency assessment is a collaborative effort. The SLP, the individual with the disorder, and sometimes their families work together to pave the way for targeted intervention and develop effective communication skills. By understanding this process, you can create characters whose journeys towards fluency feel genuine and inspiring.

Charting the Course: Treating Fluency Disorders

Fluency disorders aren't a dead end – they're challenges to be tackled with a personalized approach. Speech-Language Pathologists (SLPs) act as guides, working with individuals to craft a roadmap to smoother communication. Here's a breakdown of common treatment approaches to equip you as a writer:

The Toolbox of Speech Modification:

These strategies equip individuals with tools to manage stuttering moments and speak more fluently:

- **Slow and Steady Wins the Race:** Speaking slower allows for greater control over speech production, reducing the frequency and severity of stutters. Imagine a character taking a his time speaking, making use of pauses and breaks, allowing them to speak with measured control.
- **The Gentle Start (Easy Onset):** Starting sounds softly, like whispering the beginning of a word, helps prevent tension in the vocal cords that can trigger stuttering. Imagine a character easing into a conversation, pronouncing the first few sounds of a word delicately.
- **Relaxed Speech Production (Light Contact):** Keeping lips, tongue, and jaw relaxed minimizes tension and promotes smoother speech flow. Think of a character with a relaxed posture and open body language as they speak.
- **Pull-Out Techniques:** These strategies teach people to recognize stuttering moments and transition back to fluent speech. Imagine a character encountering a stutter, but instead of getting stuck, they use a practiced technique to regain control and continue speaking smoothly.

Building Blocks of Effective Communication:

These strategies go beyond stuttering and enhance overall speaking effectiveness:

- **The Power of the Pause:** Taking strategic breaks allows individuals to implement their fluency techniques and gather their thoughts. Imagine a character taking a moment to collect themselves before continuing their sentence.
- **Breathing Easy (Breathing Techniques):** Proper breathing (diaphragmatic breathing) helps reduce anxiety and promotes a relaxed speech pattern. Picture a character taking a deep breath from their diaphragm, filling their belly with air, before speaking.

Taming the Anxiety Monster:

Fluency disorders can be anxiety-provoking. Here are strategies to address these emotions:

- **Facing Your Fears (Desensitization):** Gradual exposure to situations that trigger anxiety can help individuals build confidence and manage their stutters. Imagine a character slowly working their way up from practicing presentations in front of a mirror to speaking in front of small groups.
- **Self-Awareness is Key (Self-Monitoring):** By recognizing their speech patterns and identifying situations that trigger stuttering, individuals can be more proactive in applying their fluency techniques. Think of a character noticing their speech quicken in stressful situations and using their "slow and steady" approach to regain control.
- **Cognitive-Behavioral Therapy (CBT):** CBT can be a valuable tool for people who stutter. This approach focuses on identifying and changing negative thoughts and beliefs associated with stuttering. By recognizing how these thoughts contribute to anxiety and avoidance behaviors around speaking, individuals can learn to challenge them and develop more realistic and empowering self-talk.

CBT can also equip individuals with coping mechanisms to manage speaking situations more confidently, leading to a reduction in stuttering frequency and an overall improvement in communication experiences.

Alternative Communication Methods (for severe cases):

In severe cases, Augmentative and Alternative Communication (AAC) tools like picture boards or speech-generating devices can support communication.

A Team Effort: Building a Support System

Fluency disorders are rarely conquered alone. A multidisciplinary approach, where a team of specialists works together, creates a stronger support system. Here's a breakdown of the key players:

Professionals

- **The Quarterback (Speech-Language Pathologists):** SLPs lead the assessment and therapy process, designing personalized treatment plans that target specific speech difficulties and communication goals.
- **The Coaches (Educators):** Teachers, counselors, and other school professionals play a crucial role. SLPs collaborate with them to develop classroom strategies and accommodations that support students with fluency disorders and help them achieve academic success.
- **The Therapist (Psychologists):** For individuals experiencing anxiety or negative emotions related to their fluency disorder, psychologists can provide valuable support with techniques to manage anxiety and develop coping mechanisms. Remember, stuttering is not an anxiety disorder, but it can create anxiety.
- **The Broader Team (Other Professionals):** Depending on the individual's needs, occupational therapists, social workers, or even medical professionals might be involved, offering specialized support to address any co-existing conditions or challenges.

The Family Circle: The Power of Support at Home

A strong support system at home is essential for progress. Here's how families contribute:

- **Knowledge is Power (Education):** Understanding fluency disorders empowers families to be more supportive and encouraging.
- **Communication Strategies:** SLPs can equip families with strategies

to facilitate smooth communication at home, creating a safe space for practicing fluency techniques.

· **Advocacy in Action:** Family members can be advocates for the individual's needs in different settings, like school or social situations.

The Benefits of Collaboration:

By working together, this team can create a comprehensive approach that addresses the various aspects of a fluency

The Stage Lights Shine Bright: Why Your Stuttering Character Can Belt Out a Tune (But Not Order Coffee)

Imagine this: Your character, Alex, dreads ordering a simple coffee. Every "c" in "cappuccino" feels like a hurdle, threatening to trip him up. Yet, later that night, he transforms on stage, belting out a powerful ballad with perfect ease. What sorcery is this?

The answer lies in the amazing adaptability of the brain. Stuttering often involves challenges in the left hemisphere, the control center for planning and coordinating speech. But when Alex sings or acts, a different region takes the wheel – the right hemisphere. Here's the breakdown:

· **Left Hemisphere:** Think of it as the "speech architect." It meticulously plans every step of speaking, from word selection to pronunciation. This planning can be a double-edged sword for someone who stutters, leading to overthinking and disfluencies.

· **Right Hemisphere:** This is the "creative maestro" of the brain. It focuses on melody, rhythm, and emotional expression. When Alex sings or acts, his right hemisphere takes over, allowing for a more automatic and emotional flow of speech. Think of it like singing along to a familiar song – the words come naturally, without getting caught up in the mechanics.

So, what does this mean for your story?

- **A Glimpse of Fluency:** Alex's experience on stage highlights the potential for fluency under certain conditions. It can add a layer of complexity to his character, showcasing his frustration with everyday speech contrasted with moments of unexpected ease.
- **Beyond the Stereotype:** This knowledge helps you avoid portraying stuttering as a simple nervous tick. It's a neurological difference, and sometimes, the right environment can unlock a hidden pathway to fluency.
- **Building on This Insight:** Maybe Alex incorporates elements of rhythm or melody into his speech therapy exercises, or finds himself singing along to music to calm his nerves before social interactions.

Remember:

- **Fluency Zones:** While singing and acting offer temporary fluency, explore "fluency zones" unique to your character. Perhaps Alex finds he speaks more easily with close friends or while engaged in a favorite activity.

By incorporating this brain science twist, you can create a more nuanced and engaging portrayal of a character who stutters. It adds depth to their struggles while offering a glimmer of hope – after all, the spotlight might not be the only place they can find their voice. A simple internet search for "Famous People Who Stutter" brings up many singers and actors for this very reason.

Debunking Myths About Fluency Disorders

Characters with communication disorders can add depth and complexity to your stories. However, fluency disorders, such as stuttering and cluttering, are often misrepresented in fiction. Here, we explore some common myths and how to portray these challenges authentically.

• **Myth: Fluency disorders equal lower intelligence.**

Reality: Fluency disorders affect how someone speaks, not how they think. A character with a stutter can be a brilliant scientist or a cunning politician. Don't conflate their communication style with their cognitive abilities.

• **Myth: Fluency disorders are a sign of laziness or lack of effort.**

Reality: These disorders are not a choice. They can be caused by neurological factors, developmental delays, or even physical limitations. Show the character's frustration and their efforts to overcome communication challenges, highlighting their determination.

• **Myth: People with fluency disorders can't communicate effectively.**

Reality: They often develop alternative strategies. Give your character creative ways to express themselves, including technology, writing, body language, or individual coping strategies.

• **Myth: Fluency disorders are temporary and everyone outgrows them.**

Reality: While some improve with therapy or over time, others are chronic. Show the challenges faced by a character who has lived with a fluency disorder for years. Explore how they navigate social interactions and advocate for themselves, demonstrating their resilience.

• **Myth: People with fluency disorders should avoid public speaking.**

Reality: With practice and support, individuals with fluency disorders can overcome anxiety and communicate effectively in public. Show a character overcoming their fear to deliver a powerful message, proving that their voice deserves to be heard.

- **Myth: Fluency disorders are "contagious" and can be "caught" by others.**

Reality: Fluency disorders are not infectious. They arise from specific underlying conditions, not imitation.

- **Myth: Telling someone to "slow down" or "take a deep breath" is helpful.**

Reality: While relaxation techniques can be part of therapy, unsolicited advice can be counterproductive. The focus should be on communication strategies that work for the individual.

- **Myth: Fluency disorders only affect speech.**

Reality: They can sometimes impact writing as well. Explore the challenges faced by a character who struggles to express themselves verbally but excels in written communication, showcasing their diverse strengths.

- **Myth: People with fluency disorders are more likely to experience anxiety or depression.**

Reality: There's no direct causal link. However, the social challenges associated with fluency disorders can contribute to anxiety or low self-esteem. Show your character navigating these challenges and building healthy coping mechanisms.

- **Myth: Fluency disorders mean a person can never have a successful career.**

Reality: Many individuals with fluency disorders thrive in a variety of professions. Explore successful characters who have overcome communication challenges, inspiring readers and challenging stereotypes.

- **Myth: Stuttering can be cured.**

Reality: There's no known cure, but effective treatment approaches can significantly improve fluency and communication skills. People who stutter can learn strategies to manage their disfluencies and communicate effectively.

- **Myth: Mastering Strategies means using them all the time.**

While speech therapy equips individuals who stutter with helpful strategies to manage disfluencies, it's a myth that these strategies can be used flawlessly all the time. Using these techniques requires ongoing practice and can be difficult in high-pressure situations or when someone feels completely comfortable and forgets or doesn't care to be mindful of their speech.

By understanding these myths, you can create characters with fluency disorders who are not defined by their communication struggles.

Portraying Fluency Disorders

Characters with fluency disorders can add depth and complexity to your stories. But ensuring their portrayal is authentic and respectful requires some key considerations. Here's a breakdown to help you create believable characters that resonate with readers:

Understanding the Nuances:

Fluency disorders aren't one-size-fits-all. Do your research!
   Speech Patterns: Explore the variations, from stuttering (repetitions, prolongations, blocks) to cluttering (rapid, disorganized speech).

Balancing Accuracy with Readability:

Realistic Speech: While incorporating disfluencies adds authenticity, avoid overloading dialogue to the point of distraction. Aim for a balance that enhances character development without sacrificing readability.

Sensitivity is Key:

- **Emotional Impact:** Fluency disorders can be emotionally challenging. Consider the internal struggles and anxieties your character might face. Again, using strategies to combat something that is always present is exhausting.
- **Compassionate Portrayal:** Show empathy and understanding. Let your characters be complex individuals with dreams, flaws, and strengths that go beyond their speech difficulties.

Breaking Stereotypes:

- **Multifaceted Characters:** Avoid clichés! Fluency disorders are just one aspect of a person's identity.
- **Respectful Representation:** Create well-rounded characters who defy stereotypes and are portrayed with dignity.
- **Debunking Myths - No Cure for Stuttering:** Therapy can manage stuttering, but there's no guaranteed "fix." Acknowledge this reality in your story to promote understanding.

Struggles and Victories:

- **Resilience in the Face of Challenges:** Show your characters navigating their difficulties with courage and determination.
- **Celebrating Triumphs:** Highlight their moments of success to inspire hope and showcase the power of perseverance.

Additional Tips:

- Consider incorporating a character's journey with therapy.
- Explore the impact of a supportive environment (family, friends) on their progress.
- Remember, fluency disorders are a communication challenge, not an intellectual disability.

By following these tips, you can create characters with fluency disorders who are authentic, relatable, and inspire empathy in your readers.

Examples

The aroma of freshly baked bread hung heavy in the air, a siren song to Ethan's stomach. He shuffled closer to the bakery window, his worn sneakers squeaking on the pavement. Inside, golden loaves sat nestled in wicker baskets, a feast for the eyes. Taking a deep breath, Ethan pushed open the door, the bell above chiming merrily.

A woman with flour-dusted cheeks beamed at him. "Welcome, dear! Can I interest you in something fresh out of the oven?"

Ethan's heart hammered in his chest. "Y-yes, please," he stammered, his voice barely a whisper. He fumbled with his backpack strap, a nervous habit.

The woman's smile faltered slightly, but she remained kind. "Wh-what can I get you, young man?" she asked, her own voice dropping a touch in an attempt to be more comfortable for him.

Ethan swallowed hard, his gaze darting between the woman and the enticing breads. His mind was a jumble, the words refusing to form on his tongue. He squeezed his eyes shut for a moment, willing himself to speak clearly. "W-wheat b-bread, p-please," he stammered, each word a struggle. "S-s-sliced," he added after a long pause, the "s" sound stretched out in a prolongation.

The woman's smile returned, wider than before. "Excellent choice," she said warmly. "Coming right up!"

Relief washed over Ethan as he waited. He tapped his foot rhythmically, another nervous tick. He hated stuttering, the way it made him feel like a malfunctioning record player, skipping and repeating (repetition). It always made him feel self-conscious, especially when interacting with strangers.

The woman returned, setting a paper bag on the counter. "There you go, one loaf of sliced wheat bread. That'll be two dollars."

Ethan fumbled for his wallet, his fingers trembling slightly. He hated this part too, the fumbling and the worried glances he always received. "Um, um," he filled the silence with nervous filler words before finally managing, "Here you go."

The woman noticed his struggle and leaned closer, her voice dropping to a gentle murmur. "Take your time, dear. No rush."

Ethan met her gaze, surprised by the understanding in her eyes. A small smile tugged at his lips. "Th-thank you," he managed, feeling a flicker of warmth spread through him. He placed the exact amount on the counter.

The woman rang him up, her movements slow and deliberate. "You have a kind heart, young man," she said, handing him his receipt.

Ethan blinked, surprised. "Me?" he stammered, a block interrupting his initial question.

The woman winked. "The way you looked at those loaves, like they were pure gold. That's a kind heart right there."

Ethan stared at her, speechless for a moment. He hadn't expected that, not at all. Then, a genuine smile spread across his face, chasing away the self-consciousness. "Th-thank you," he said again, sincerity ringing in his voice.

He walked out of the bakery, the paper bag warm in his hand. He didn't just have bread; he had a newfound confidence, a flicker of hope that maybe, just maybe, people could see beyond the stutter and recognize the person beneath it.

Here are some things to keep in mind when writing dialogue for a character who stutters:

Accuracy and Respect:

- **Research:** Familiarize yourself with different types of stuttering (repetitions, blocks, prolongations) and their impact on speech.
- **Sensitivity:** Avoid portraying stuttering as a joke or making fun of the character.
- **Focus on Character:** Let the stutter be a part of the character, not their defining trait. Highlight their personality and strengths.

Techniques:

- **Variety:** Use a combination of repetitions, blocks (silent pauses), prolongations (stretching sounds), and interjections ("um," "uh") to create a realistic portrayal.
- **Severity:** Adjust the frequency and intensity of the stuttering based on the character's comfort level and the situation. Stressful situations might increase stuttering.
- **Context:** Consider how the character's stutter might affect their word choice. They might avoid complex words or rephrase sentences to avoid problematic sounds.

Readability:

- **Balance:** Strive for a balance between realism and readability. Too much stuttering can be frustrating for readers.
- **Clarity:** Don't sacrifice clarity for accuracy. Ensure the overall meaning of the dialogue remains clear.
- **Flow:** Read the dialogue aloud to ensure it flows naturally despite the stuttering.

Additional tips:

- **Show, Don't Tell:** Instead of explicitly stating the character is stuttering, use descriptive language to convey the struggle (e.g., "Ethan squeezed his eyes shut for a moment, willing himself to speak clearly").
- **Body Language:** Incorporate nervous habits like foot tapping or hand fidgeting to show the character's internal struggle.
- **Positive Representation:** Show the character overcoming challenges or connecting with others despite their stutter. Even better, show them as a whole person with the stutter only one part of their description.

By following these tips, you can write dialogue for a character who stutters that is both realistic and respectful, adding depth and complexity to your story.

The Final Word: Creating Inclusive Characters with Fluency Disorders

Writing characters with fluency disorders goes beyond simply including stutters. Here's a final thought to leave you with:

- **Respectful Portrayal:** Authenticity and respect go hand-in-hand. Research the complexities of speech patterns (stuttering, cluttering) to avoid stereotypes and create believable characters. Here's the key: Don't let the stutter define the person.
- **Treat it like any other physical characteristic.** For example, if your character has red hair or freckles, you wouldn't dwell on it constantly. It's simply a part of who they are. Similarly, weave the stutter into the character's background and personality, but don't let it overshadow their strengths and dreams.
- **Highlight their individuality.** Does your character who stutters love to play guitar? Are they a whiz at baking? Are they known for their dry wit? Showcase these other facets of their personality to create a well-rounded

person, not just someone defined by their speech pattern.

- **Balancing Readability with Realism:** While incorporating disfluencies adds a realistic touch, don't overload dialogue to the point of distraction. Aim for a balance that enhances character development and keeps the story flowing.
- **Challenging Misconceptions:** Debunk myths like the idea of a "cure" for stuttering. This promotes understanding and acceptance of fluency disorders in real life.

The Power of Storytelling:

Authors have the power to shape perceptions and foster empathy. By creating characters with fluency disorders who are well-rounded, relatable, and courageous, you can contribute to a more inclusive society.

Remember: Fluency disorders are a communication challenge, not an intellectual or emotional disability. Your characters can have dreams, flaws, and strengths that extend far beyond their speech.

Empowering Diverse Voices:

Embrace the opportunity to showcase diversity and complexity in your writing. By including characters with fluency disorders, you contribute to a richer literary landscape and promote understanding and acceptance in the real world.

For more information:

- **National Stuttering Association:** https://westutter.org/
- **The Stuttering Foundation:** https://www.stutteringhelp.org/
- **American Speech Language Hearing Association:** https://www.asha.org/public/speech/disorders/stuttering/
- **John Hopkins Medicine:** https://www.hopkinsmedicine.org/health/conditions-and-diseases/fluency-disorder

- **Please Let Me Finish My Sentence:** https://youtu.be/-TsPPbRGHbk? si=VMUkv_KgnpTz8qmS
- **I Don't Need to Be Fixed: What I Wish the World Knew About Stuttering:** https://youtu.be/GgMqvvjhxQc?si=AQWQB0ZkQbBH8HGl
- **Mayo Clinic:** https://www.mayoclinic.org/diseases-conditions/stutteri ng/symptoms-causes/syc-20353572

Character Checklist: Fluency Disorders (Stuttering, Cluttering)

This checklist is designed to help you develop a character with a fluency disorder in a sensitive and authentic way.

Character Background:

- Specific Fluency Disorder: Does your character have stuttering, cluttering, or another fluency disorder?
- Age of Onset: When did the fluency disorder develop (childhood, adulthood)? Was there a triggering event?
- Diagnosis: When were they diagnosed? By who? What was the assessor's attitude toward their disorder? How did the character feel about the diagnosis?
- Severity: How severe is the fluency disorder? Does it mildly disrupt speech or significantly impact communication?
- Cause/trigger (if known): Is there a known cause or triggering incident for the fluency disorder (e.g., neurological condition, anxiety)?

Speech Characteristics:

- Stuttering: If applicable, what are the specific characteristics of your character's stutter (blocks, repetitions, prolongations)?
- Cluttering: If applicable, how does your character's cluttering manifest (rapid speech rate, sound omissions, revisions)?

- Filler Words: Does your character use filler words ("um," "like") more frequently to manage their disfluencies?

Communication Strategies:

- Self-Monitoring: Is your character aware of their disfluencies? Do they try to control them or avoid certain words/situations?
- Coping Mechanisms: What coping mechanisms does your character use to manage their fluency disorder (deep breaths, eye contact)?
- Speech Therapy: Has your character received speech therapy? If so, how has it impacted their fluency?

Emotional Impact:

- Frustration: Does your character experience frustration or embarrassment due to their fluency disorder?
- Isolation: Does the fluency disorder lead to social isolation or difficulty making friends?
- Confidence: How does the fluency disorder impact your character's self-confidence and communication skills?
- Discrimination: Has your character experienced discrimination or negative reactions because of their speech?

Additional Considerations:

- Support System: Does your character have a supportive family, friends, or teachers who understand their fluency disorder?
- Impact on Relationships: How does the fluency disorder affect your character's romantic or professional relationships?
- Character Development: How does the fluency disorder shape your character's personality, goals, and self-advocacy?

Narrative Choices:

- Dialogue: How will you represent your character's disfluencies in writing (italics, dashes, phonetic sounds)?
- Internal Monologue: Will you use internal monologue to explore your character's thoughts and anxieties around their speech?
- Balance: Have you balanced authenticity with the need for clear and engaging storytelling.

Character Development:

- Strengths and Struggles: How does your character's fluency disorder impact their daily life and interactions with others?
- Beyond Speech: What are your character's strengths and personality traits beyond their fluency disorder?
- Avoid Stereotypes: Have you avoided relying solely on their fluency disorder to define your character?
- Inclusion of options: Have you given your character options for treatment and coping?

Representation:

- Respectful Portrayal: Have you portrayed your character's fluency disorder with respect and sensitivity?
- Avoidance of Caricatures: Have you avoided stereotypical or exaggerated representations of people who stutter or cluttering?

Remember:

- This checklist is a starting point; not all characters with fluency disorders will experience all of these aspects.
- Research the specific fluency disorder to ensure an accurate portrayal.
- Consider including resources for readers who want to learn more.

- Focus on your character's unique voice, resilience, and strengths, not just their communication challenges.

Challenge Accepted? Stuttering for a Day to Deepen Your Characters

Crafting characters with fluency disorders requires empathy and understanding. While research is crucial, there's no substitute for experiencing a communication challenge firsthand. So, here's a bold proposition: **try stuttering for a day.**

Yes, you read that right. For 24 hours, consciously interject stuttered sounds ("b-b-book," "m-m-may I") or prolong syllables ("thhhhank you") into your speech. It won't perfectly replicate the complexities of a fluency disorder, but it can offer a glimpse into the frustrations and challenges faced by those who experience them daily.

You will be changing your speech much like therapy works to change those with fluency disorders.

Why Stutter for a Day?

- Empathy Through Experience: This exercise isn't about mockery. It's about stepping outside your comfort zone to understand the emotional impact of a fluency disorder.
- Beyond Stereotypes: Stuttering often gets reduced to a nervous tick in fiction. This challenge can help you create a more nuanced and realistic portrayal.
- Respectful Representation: By experiencing the frustration of disfluency, you gain a deeper respect for the resilience and communication strategies people with fluency disorders develop.

Important Considerations:

- Sensitivity: This challenge is meant to be a learning experience, not a mockery. Be mindful of the realities of fluency disorders and avoid perpetuating stereotypes.
- Safety and Comfort: If you have any pre-existing speech conditions, consult a doctor before attempting this exercise. Stop if you feel uncomfortable or frustrated.
- Focus on Communication: Remember, the goal is to understand the communication challenges, not to become a flawless impersonator.

The Power of Vulnerability

This challenge isn't about perfection. It's about opening yourself up to a new perspective. By experiencing the frustration of disfluency, even for a day, you can develop a deeper understanding of the characters you create. This empathy will translate into richer, more authentic portrayals, and ensure your characters with fluency disorders are not defined by their communication struggles, but by their strength and resilience.

Are you ready to accept the challenge?

6

Voice Disorders:

When the Instrument Falters

T he human voice is a powerful tool. It allows us to connect, express ourselves, and navigate the world around us. But what happens when this instrument falters? Voice disorders disrupt the smooth production of sound, impacting how we communicate and interact with others. This chapter delves into the complexities of voice disorders, equipping you as an author to craft characters whose struggles and triumphs with their voice feel genuine and relatable.

At its core, a voice disorder is a disturbance in the way your vocal folds (the two folds of tissue in your larynx that vibrate to produce sound) function. This malfunction can be caused by a variety of factors, from structural abnormalities in the vocal folds themselves to neurological conditions or even overuse. The result? A disruption in the quality, pitch, and resonance of your voice.

Imagine your voice as a finely tuned instrument. Voice quality refers to the overall "cleanness" of the sound – a healthy voice sounds clear and smooth. Disorders can introduce distortions like hoarseness, breathiness, or roughness, making the voice sound strained or raspy. Pitch, on the other hand, is the highness or lowness of your voice. Voice disorders can cause your voice to pitch abnormally high or low, affecting your vocal range and expressiveness. Finally, resonance refers to the way sound vibrates within your body and projects outwards. Imagine a singer with a powerful, resonant voice that fills the room. Voice disorders can alter this resonance, making your voice sound muffled or weak.

By understanding these disruptions, you can create characters whose voice struggles feel authentic. The next sections will explore the various types of voice disorders, their causes, and the impact they can have on an individual's life. We'll also delve into treatment options and strategies for managing these challenges. So, let's turn the page and embark on a journey into the world of voice disorders.

Please note:

The information presented in this book is intended to provide writers with a general understanding of communication disorders. It is not a replacement for a professional evaluation by a qualified Speech–Language Pathologist (SLP). If you suspect someone may have a communication disorder, please consult with an SLP for diagnosis and treatment recommendations.

Types of Voice Disorders

The human voice is a delicate instrument, and just like any instrument, it can be susceptible to malfunctions. These malfunctions manifest as various voice disorders, each with its unique characteristics and impact on an author's character. There are several types of voice disorders.

Structural Voice Disorders: When the Instrument Breaks

Let's delve into some of the most common structural disorders that can affect the vocal folds:

- **Nodules:** Imagine a singer straining their voice night after night. Over time, these repeated stresses can lead to the formation of calluses on their vocal folds – these are nodules. Nodules are like tiny bumps that develop from vocal abuse or misuse, such as constantly yelling or speaking in a strained voice.

- **Polyps:** Similarly, polyps are fluid-filled sacs, like blisters, that can form on the vocal folds due to overuse or irritation.

Both nodules and polyps can cause hoarseness, breathiness, and vocal fatigue. Imagine your character's voice becoming increasingly raspy and weak as they struggle to maintain volume or pitch.

- **Cysts:** Vocal fold cysts are like little hidden pockets of fluid that can develop within the tissue.
- **Reinke's Edema:** Reinke's edema, on the other hand, is a more general swelling of the vocal folds caused by chronic irritation.

Both conditions can lead to a thickening of the vocal folds, resulting in a muffled or breathy voice. Characters with these disorders might sound like they're constantly congested or having difficulty pushing sound out.

- **Granulomas:** Granulomas are inflammatory bumps that form on the surface of the vocal folds, often in response to irritation or trauma.
- **Sulcus vocalis:** This is a furrow or groove that develops along the length of the fold, thinning the tissue.

Both conditions can cause voice changes like hoarseness and vocal fatigue. Imagine a character who constantly feels a tickle in their throat or gets hoarse easily after extended periods of talking.

- **Scarring:** Vocal fold scarring can occur due to trauma, surgery, or even inflammation. This scarring can leave the vocal folds stiff and less flexible, impacting their ability to vibrate properly.
- **Damage or removal:** While this is less common, can also significantly alter voice production.

Characters with these conditions might have a permanently hoarse or breathy voice, or they might struggle to speak loudly or with a full range of pitch.

It's important to remember that these are just some of the many structural disorders that can affect the voice. The severity and treatment options will vary depending on the specific condition. The key takeaway for authors is to understand how these disorders can impact the sound and quality of a character's voice, allowing for a more realistic and nuanced portrayal.

Neurological Voice Disorders: When the Brain Can't Quite Find the Tune

The human voice is a complex system, and sometimes the messages from the brain get scrambled. Neurological voice disorders arise when issues in the nervous system disrupt the delicate control of the vocal folds, impacting how we speak. Let's explore some common culprits that can turn a character's voice from smooth to strained:

- **Spasmodic Dysphonia: The Unruly Vocal Folds:** Imagine a character trying to tell a story, but their voice keeps breaking or trembling mid-sentence. This could be Spasmodic Dysphonia, a condition where the brain sends involuntary "spams" to the vocal folds, causing strained or interrupted speech. Characters with this disorder might sound like they're constantly catching their breath or struggling to push words out.
- **Vocal Fold Paralysis and Paresis: A Loss of Connection:** When nerves connecting to the vocal folds are damaged, it can lead to paralysis (complete immobility) or paresis (weakness) in these muscles. This can cause breathiness, hoarseness, and difficulty controlling pitch and volume. Imagine a character who used to have a booming voice but now sounds weak and breathy, struggling to project or speak loudly.
- **Vocal Tremors, Spasms, and Dystonia: When Control Goes Awry:** Several neurological conditions can cause involuntary movements in the vocal folds. Vocal cord tremors create a shaky or quivering voice

quality. Vocal cord spasms might interrupt speech with sudden breaks or pitch fluctuations. Vocal fold dystonia can cause a combination of tremors, pitch breaks, and difficulty controlling the voice. Characters with these conditions might sound like their voice is wobbling, catching, or struggling to stay steady.

- **Myoclonus: The Hiccups of the Voice Box:** Imagine having hiccups, but instead of your diaphragm, it's your vocal folds that keep having quick, repetitive spasms. This is Vocal Fold Myoclonus, causing abrupt interruptions or jerky movements during speech. It can make a character's voice sound irregular and disrupt the flow of their speech.
- **Breathing: The Invisible Partner in Voice:** Just like any instrument needs air to produce sound, so do our vocal folds. Disruptions in breathing patterns can significantly impact voice quality.
- **Shallow breathing,** where someone primarily uses chest muscles instead of the diaphragm, can lead to breathiness and reduced vocal projection.
- **Breath holding** can cause voice breaks or a strained quality.
- **Irregular breathing** patterns can make speech sound rushed or hesitant.
- **Inefficient breath support,** often due to weak respiratory muscles, can result in breathiness, vocal fatigue, or inconsistent volume.

Paradoxical Vocal Fold Movement (PVFM) and Vocal Cord Dysfunction (VCD): When the Folds Misbehave

These two conditions involve abnormal movements of the vocal folds during breathing or speaking.

PVFM can cause stridor (a whistling sound during inhalation) or voice breaks, while **VCD** can lead to breathiness, difficulty initiating speech, or a strained voice quality. Imagine a character who constantly sounds wheezy or struggles to catch their breath while talking, even when they're not physically exerting themselves.

Understanding these neurological conditions allows you to craft characters whose voice struggles feel real and relatable. The next section will delve into other factors that can contribute to voice disorders, giving you a well-rounded picture for your characters' vocal journeys.

The Silent Struggle: Understanding Selective Mutism

While not strictly a voice disorder, selective mutism is an important condition to consider for creating well-rounded characters who face challenges with communication.

It's a complex situation where individuals, despite having the physical ability to speak, are unable or unwilling to do so in certain settings or with specific people. This condition often begins in childhood and can persist if left unaddressed.

The Grip of Anxiety:

At the heart of selective mutism often lies anxiety. Social situations can be incredibly overwhelming for individuals with this condition, leading to a freeze response where speaking becomes impossible.

Imagine a character who thrives in quiet environments with familiar faces but clams up entirely in a crowded classroom. This silence can create significant challenges in academic, social, and professional settings, hindering their ability to connect with others. Selective mutism can sometimes co-occur with underlying anxiety disorders, social phobia, or past traumas.

Finding Their Voice Again:

The good news is that selective mutism is treatable. Treatment typically involves a team effort from a therapist, speech-language pathologist (SLP), and often the family.

Cognitive-behavioral therapy (CBT) helps individuals identify and manage their anxiety, building confidence in their communication skills.

Speech therapy equips them with tools and strategies to overcome communication barriers. Imagine a character working with an SLP to practice relaxation techniques before social interactions or learning alternative communication methods like picture cards.

Family involvement is also crucial.

Creating a supportive and understanding environment at home fosters a safe space for the individual to practice communication and build the courage to use their voice in a wider range of situations. With comprehensive treatment and support, characters with selective mutism can develop the skills and confidence to break free from their silence and participate more fully in the world around them.

Why Voices Go Awry: Exploring the Causes of Voice Disorders

The human voice is a resilient instrument, but even the sturdiest instruments can be affected by wear and tear, or even external factors. Understanding the various causes of voice disorders equips you as an author to craft characters whose voice struggles feel genuine. Let's delve into the culprits that can turn a booming voice into a whisper:

Vocal Misuse and Abuse: Singing in the Shower Can Turn Sour

Imagine your character, a passionate sports coach, constantly yelling instructions at practice. Over time, this overuse and strain can lead to vocal misuse and abuse, a major culprit behind voice disorders.

This includes shouting, screaming, speaking in loud environments for extended periods, or simply not using proper vocal techniques. All this vocal strain can inflame and fatigue the vocal folds, eventually leading to hoarseness or even vocal fold damage.

Making Matters Worse: Excessive Use and Bad Habits

Just like any muscle, the voice needs rest and proper care. Characters who use their voice excessively without giving it time to recover, or those with bad habits like smoking or constantly clearing their throats, are more likely to experience voice problems.

Think of an enthusiastic salesperson who talks all day without breaks, or a singer who constantly pushes their voice to hit high notes – both are at risk of vocal strain and potential damage.

The Workplace and Environment: From Construction Sites to Rock Concerts

Certain professions and environments can put a strain on your voice. Construction workers in loud environments or singers performing in smoky rock concerts are constantly exposed to noise that can take a toll on their vocal folds.

Similarly, occupations with high vocal demands, like teachers or public speakers, can lead to vocal fatigue if proper vocal hygiene practices aren't followed.

GERD: When Stomach Acid Takes a Wrong Turn

Gastroesophageal Reflux Disease, or GERD, is a condition where stomach acid creeps up into the esophagus, irritating the throat and vocal folds.

Chronic acid reflux can inflame and damage the vocal folds, contributing to voice disorders like laryngitis or vocal fold nodules. Imagine a character who constantly has heartburn – the irritation caused by the acid reflux can also affect their voice quality.

The Brain-Voice Connection: When Neurology Gets Disrupted

Sometimes, the problem lies not in the vocal folds themselves, but in the messages they receive from the brain. Neurological conditions that damage nerves or muscles involved in vocal fold movement can lead to changes in voice quality, pitch, or volume.

Conditions like Parkinson's disease or stroke can affect the brain's control over the vocal mechanism, resulting in voice disturbances.

Structural Issues: When the Instrument Has Flaws

Structural abnormalities in the vocal folds, whether present at birth (congenital) or acquired later in life (lesions), can also predispose someone to voice disorders. These abnormalities can affect how the vocal folds vibrate and produce sound, leading to voice changes and difficulty speaking.

Laryngectomy: A Necessary but Life-Altering Surgery

In some cases, the larynx (voice box) itself might need to be removed, either partially or completely. This procedure, called a laryngectomy, is often performed to treat advanced laryngeal cancer or other severe conditions.

A **total laryngectomy** removes the entire larynx, including the vocal folds, permanently eliminating natural speech. Characters who undergo this surgery require alternative methods of communication, such as esophageal speech or voice prosthetics.

A **partial laryngectomy** attempts to preserve some vocal function by removing only a portion of the larynx. While this approach aims to maintain some natural speaking ability, it can still result in changes to voice quality and swallowing function.

By understanding these diverse causes, you can create characters whose voice struggles feel authentic and believable. The next section will explore how these voice disorders manifest themselves, giving you a well-rounded picture for your characters' vocal journeys.

When Your Voice Betrays You: Manifestations and Impact of Voice Disorders

A healthy voice is our connection to the world. It allows us to express ourselves, share ideas, and build relationships. But what happens when that connection falters? Voice disorders manifest in a variety of ways, each impacting how a character communicates and interacts with the world around them.

The Many Faces of Vocal Trouble: Symptoms and Characteristics

Hoarseness: Imagine a character who used to be a captivating storyteller, but now their voice sounds rough and strained – this is hoarseness, a hallmark symptom of many voice disorders.

Hoarseness is caused by irregular vibration of the vocal folds, resulting in that raspy quality. Another character might constantly sound breathy, like they're whispering even when they're trying to project. This is due to incomplete closure of the vocal folds, causing air to leak during speech.

Other common symptoms include:

- **Strain:** Imagine a character who sounds tense and struggles to get words out. This is vocal strain, caused by excessive effort in the vocal mechanism.
- **Pitch Changes:** A character's voice might fluctuate in pitch, or even crack mid-sentence due to vocal fold irregularities.
- **Glottal Attacks:** Sudden, harsh vocal onsets can occur when the vocal folds slam shut too forcefully at the beginning of speech.
- **Voice Breaks:** Imagine a character's voice cutting out entirely for a moment – this is a voice break, a disruption in vocal production.

- **Pain:** Throat soreness or discomfort can accompany vocal strain or inflammation.
- **Vocal Fry:** This is that low, creaky sound sometimes used for emphasis, but it can also be a sign of vocal fatigue. Imagine a character who constantly sounds like they're whispering, even at normal volume.

The severity and persistence of these symptoms can vary greatly. Some characters might experience mild hoarseness occasionally, while others might face chronic voice problems that significantly impact their daily lives. Factors like the underlying cause, individual vocal anatomy, and treatment effectiveness all play a role in how a character's voice disorder manifests.

Beyond the Physical: The Ripple Effect of Voice Disorders

The impact of a voice disorder goes far beyond just sounding different. It can significantly affect a character's communication, social interactions, and even their emotional well-being.

- **Communication Challenges:** Imagine a character struggling to be heard or understood due to their voice problems. This can lead to frustration and difficulty conveying messages clearly.
- **Social Struggles:** Social settings can become a minefield for characters with voice disorders. Participating in conversations, ordering food at a restaurant, or even making a phone call can feel overwhelming.
- **Professional Impact:** For characters in professions that rely heavily on vocal communication, such as teachers, lawyers, or singers, a voice disorder can be a significant career barrier.
- **Emotional Toll:** Living with a voice disorder can take an emotional toll. Characters might experience frustration, embarrassment, and anxiety about their voice and how it's perceived by others.

Understanding these manifestations and their impact allows you to create characters whose voice struggles feel real and relatable. The next section will explore how these disorders are diagnosed and treated, giving you the tools to show how your characters navigate their vocal journeys.

Cracking the Case: Unveiling Voice Disorders Through Diagnosis

Imagine a character struggling with their voice, but not knowing why. Diagnosing a voice disorder is like solving a mystery – healthcare professionals work together to gather clues and identify the culprit behind the vocal struggles. Understanding this process equips you to craft characters whose journeys towards vocal health feel authentic.

Assembling the Puzzle Pieces: The Evaluation Process

A team effort is key to diagnosing voice disorders. Otolaryngologists (ear, nose, and throat specialists) team up with speech-language pathologists (SLPs) to get a complete picture. The evaluation might involve:

- **Case History:** This is where your character spills the beans – their medical history, vocal habits, work environment, and any changes they've noticed in their voice.
- **Physical Examination:** Just like a mechanic looking under the hood, a doctor will examine the vocal folds to check for abnormalities or signs of trouble.
- **Instrumental Assessment:** Just like a mechanic uses specialized tools to diagnose a car problem, healthcare professionals have a toolbox of instruments to assess vocal function in intricate detail.

These tools provide valuable insights into how your character's vocal folds are vibrating, how air is flowing through the vocal tract, and the acoustic characteristics of their voice. Let's delve deeper into this vocal detective work:

Laryngoscopy: A Direct Look Inside

Imagine a tiny camera, about the size of a straw, being gently inserted through the nose or mouth to reach the larynx (voice box).

This is laryngoscopy, offering a real-time view of the vocal folds vibrating during speech. It allows doctors to see any abnormalities in the structure or movement of the vocal folds, such as nodules, polyps, or inflammation.

Stroboscopy: Slow-Motion Replay for Vocal Folds

Stroboscopy takes laryngoscopy a step further. By using a special light source that flashes in coordination with the vocal fold vibrations, stroboscopy creates a slow-motion effect.

This allows doctors to see subtle details of vocal fold movement, helping them identify irregularities in vibration patterns that contribute to voice problems. Imagine being able to see exactly how smoothly (or not so smoothly) your character's vocal folds are coming together with each sound they produce.

Acoustic Analysis: Decoding the Soundscape of Speech

Our voices aren't just a single note – they're a complex blend of frequencies that determine pitch, loudness, and overall quality. Acoustic analysis uses specialized software to measure these various acoustic characteristics of your character's voice.

This can reveal issues like breathiness, hoarseness, or vocal strain by analyzing things like pitch variations, sound intensity, and the presence of noise within the voice signal.

Aerodynamic Testing: Measuring the Breath Behind the Voice

Just like a fire needs air to burn, our vocal folds need airflow to vibrate and produce sound. Aerodynamic testing measures the airflow and pressure within the vocal tract during speech. This helps doctors assess how efficiently your character is using their breath to support their voice, and identify any issues with airflow that might be contributing to vocal strain or breathiness.

Spectrogram: A Voice Fingerprint

Imagine a visual representation of your character's voice – that's a spectrogram. This instrument creates a graph that shows the frequency and time of the sound waves produced by the vocal folds. By analyzing the spectrogram, doctors can gain insights into the overall health of the vocal folds and identify any abnormalities that might be affecting voice quality. Think of it like a fingerprint for your voice, revealing unique characteristics and any areas that might need attention.

Perceptual Evaluation: The Art of Listening to the Voice

While the instrumental assessments offer a glimpse into the mechanics of your character's voice, perceptual evaluation focuses on the end product – the sound itself.

Imagine a concert sound technician with a finely tuned ear, meticulously adjusting dials to create the perfect acoustics.

In this case, the sound technician is a trained professional, often a speech-language pathologist (SLP), who uses their expertise to assess the quality and characteristics of your character's voice.

This evaluation goes beyond simply listening. The SLP will likely employ a standardized rating scale to systematically assess various aspects of your character's vocal quality. Here's a breakdown of some key areas they might focus on:

- **Pitch:** Is your character's voice too high, too low, or does it strain to reach certain notes? The SLP will evaluate their overall pitch range and any pitch breaks or fluctuations that might indicate vocal strain or weakness.
- **Loudness:** Can your character project their voice clearly, or do they struggle to be heard? The SLP will assess their overall volume and their ability to modulate loudness effectively.
- **Longevity:** How long can your character sustain phonation (voice production) without experiencing vocal fatigue or strain? The SLP will evaluate their ability to speak for extended periods without vocal breaks or quality deterioration.
- **Quality:** This is where things get interesting. The SLP will listen closely for any deviations from a healthy vocal quality, such as breathiness, hoarseness, strain, nasality, or vocal fry.

They'll also assess aspects like breath support, resonance (the way sound resonates within the vocal tract), and overall clarity of speech.

By combining this detailed perceptual evaluation with the insights gained from instrumental assessments, healthcare professionals can create a well-rounded picture of your character's vocal health.

This information is vital for not only diagnosing the underlying cause of their voice disorder but also for guiding treatment decisions and monitoring progress over time. The next section will explore the various treatment options available to help characters reclaim their voice and speak with confidence.

The SLP: Your Character's Voice Champion

Speech-language pathologists (SLPs) are like vocal coaches for people with voice disorders. They play a key role in assessment, treatment, and rehabilitation. Collaboration between otolaryngologists and SLPs ensures a well-rounded approach, tailoring treatment to your character's specific needs.

Sifting Through the Possibilities: Differential Diagnosis

Not all voice problems are created equal. Doctors need to differentiate between different types of voice disorders and identify the underlying cause. This might involve ruling out other medical conditions that could be affecting the voice, such as:

- Laryngitis (inflammation of the voice box)
- Vocal fold nodules or polyps (growths on the vocal folds)
- Vocal cord paralysis (loss of movement in the vocal folds)
- Muscle tension dysphonia (vocal strain due to muscle tension)
- Benign vocal fold lesions (non-cancerous growths)

Looking at the Bigger Picture: Co-existing Conditions

Sometimes, voice problems don't exist in a vacuum. They can co-occur with other medical or communication conditions, like:

- GERD (acid reflux)
- Allergies
- Respiratory infections
- Neurological disorders
- Psychological factors

Considering these co-existing conditions allows for a more comprehensive treatment plan, addressing all the contributing factors impacting your character's voice.

By understanding the evaluation and diagnosis process, you can create characters whose voice struggles feel real and believable. The next section will delve into the various treatment options available, giving you the tools to show how your characters can reclaim their voice.

Finding Their Voice Again: Treatment and Intervention Approaches for Voice Disorders

Imagine a character who's lost their voice, or whose voice has become a source of frustration. The journey towards vocal recovery is a unique one for each character, but understanding the treatment options equips you to craft a believable path to regaining their voice.

Voice Therapy: Retraining the Instrument

Just like any skilled musician, the voice benefits from training. This is where a speech-language pathologist (SLP) steps in, acting as a vocal coach for your character. Voice therapy involves a series of exercises and strategies designed to:

- **Strengthen Breath Support:** Think of breath as the fuel for the voice. Therapy can help your character improve how they control their breath, providing a strong foundation for clear and effortless speech.
- **Enhance Vocal Resonance:** Imagine the space where your voice seems to vibrate – that's resonance. Therapy can help your character optimize resonance for a richer and more powerful voice.
- **Improve Articulation:** Clear speech relies on precise movements of the tongue, lips, and jaw. Therapy can help your character refine their articulation for better intelligibility.
- **Reduce Vocal Strain:** Bad vocal habits can lead to strain and fatigue. Therapy can equip your character with techniques to use their voice

safely and efficiently.

- **Promote Vocal Hygiene:** Just like taking care of your teeth, vocal hygiene is essential. Therapy can teach your character practices like proper hydration, vocal rest, and avoiding irritants to keep their voice healthy.

Rehabilitation Exercises: Building Vocal Stamina

Think of a runner training for a marathon – vocal rehabilitation exercises work similarly. These exercises aim to strengthen and condition the vocal folds, improving your character's vocal endurance and resilience. This can help them speak for extended periods without experiencing fatigue or strain.

Medical and Surgical Interventions: Addressing the Root Cause

Sometimes, the problem goes beyond vocal technique. In cases where voice disorders stem from structural abnormalities or medical conditions, medical or surgical interventions might be necessary. This could involve procedures like:

- **Vocal Fold Surgery:** Imagine repairing a damaged vocal fold, like fixing a torn ligament. This surgery can address structural issues affecting vocal function.
- **Botox Injections:** For characters with muscle spasms or paralysis affecting their vocal folds, botox injections can offer temporary relief. Think of a targeted treatment to relax muscles and improve vocal control.

Medications: Lending a Helping Hand

Medications can play a supporting role in voice treatment. Depending on the underlying cause, characters might benefit from:

- **Steroids:** To reduce inflammation in the vocal folds.

- **Antibiotics:** To address infections contributing to voice problems.
- **Antireflux medications:** For characters with GERD, managing acid reflux can significantly improve vocal health.

You are absolutely right! An SGD (Speech-Generating Device) is a type of AAC (Augmentative and Alternative Communication) system.

I apologize for the oversight in the previous text. I will update it to reflect this accuracy. Here's the corrected version:

Communication Options for Characters After Laryngectomy

The Silent Struggle:

Losing one's voice due to laryngectomy can be a life-altering experience for your character. Not only do they face physical challenges, but their ability to communicate and connect with others is significantly impacted.

Beyond Silence: Restoring Communication

Fortunately, there are several options that can help your character regain their voice and express themselves. Here's a breakdown of some popular methods to consider:

Electrolarynx (Electronic Artificial Larynx):

- **Function:** This handheld device vibrates against the throat or placed in the mouth, creating a buzzing sound. Characters can then mouth words to form speech.
- **Benefits:** Offers immediate voice restoration, requires minimal maintenance.
- **Drawbacks:** The synthesized voice can sound robotic, and the device can malfunction.
- **Character Portrayal:** This can be a quick solution for characters who need

a voice right away, but highlight the limitations through the mechanical quality of the speech.

Tracheoesophageal Voice Prosthesis (TEVP):

- **Function:** A surgical procedure creates a connection between the windpipe (trachea) and the esophagus. A one-way valve and external voice prosthesis allow air to flow into the esophagus, creating vibrations that mimic vocal cord function.
- **Benefits:** More natural-sounding voice compared to electrolarynx, requires less frequent maintenance.
- **Drawbacks:** Requires surgery, characters need to cover their stoma (tracheostomy opening) while speaking (hands-free valves are an option for some).
- **Character Portrayal:** This can offer a more natural-sounding voice, but incorporate the need to cover the stoma or the existence of hands-free valves.

Esophageal Speech:

- **Function:** A technique where characters learn to swallow air into the esophagus and control its expulsion to create vibrations for speech production.
- **Benefits:** Offers the potential for natural-sounding speech, doesn't require any external devices.
- **Drawbacks:** Requires significant practice and dedication to master, speech may be limited in volume and duration.
- **Character Portrayal:** This can offer a natural-sounding voice but emphasize the effort and limitations involved.

Speech-Generating Devices (SGDs), an AAC option:

- **Function:** Electronic devices that allow characters to select pre-recorded phrases or type words that are then synthesized into speech.
- **Benefits:** A valuable tool for characters who cannot speak at all, offers portability and variety in communication options.
- **Drawbacks:** Doesn't allow for natural speech or expression of emotions through tone.
- **Character Portrayal:** This can be a useful tool for characters who struggle with other methods, but highlight the limitations of pre-recorded phrases and lack of natural inflection.

Sign Language, another AAC option

- **Function:** A complete and complex language using hand gestures and facial expressions for communication.
- **Benefits:** Natural and expressive, doesn't require any devices, can foster connection with the Deaf community.
- **Drawbacks:** Requires dedication and time to learn, limited accessibility depending on the environment and knowledge of others.
- **Character Portrayal:** This can be a rich and rewarding communication option, but acknowledge the learning curve and potential social barriers.

The Choice is Yours

The best communication method for your character depends on their personality, situation, and the story you want to tell. Consider these options:

- **Physical Capabilities:** Can your character undergo surgery? How much practice and coordination do they have?
- **Social Environment:** How familiar are those around them with different communication methods?
- **Character Arc:** How does losing their voice impact them? Does regaining communication play a role in their journey?

Remember:

- **Emotional Impact:** Losing one's voice can be a deeply emotional experience. Explore the character's feelings of isolation, frustration, or determination.
- **Adaptation and Resilience:** Show how your character adapts to their new reality and finds ways to connect with the world.
- **Beyond Words:** Communication isn't just about spoken language. Explore facial expressions, body language, and alternative methods your character might develop.

By incorporating these communication options thoughtfully, you can create a rich and believable character who overcomes the challenges of laryngectomy and finds their voice in a new way.

Prevention - Vocal Hygiene

Vocal hygiene, just like good oral hygiene, is essential for maintaining a healthy and powerful voice. This involves practices that keep your vocal cords lubricated and prevent strain.

- Drinking plenty of water throughout the day keeps your vocal cords hydrated and reduces irritation. Limiting alcohol and caffeine, which can dehydrate your body, is also important.
- Avoiding excessive throat clearing, yelling, or straining your voice can prevent inflammation and damage.
- Warming up your voice with gentle stretches and humming before strenuous use helps prepare your vocal cords for optimal performance.

By practicing good vocal hygiene, you can ensure your voice stays clear, strong, and ready to communicate effectively.

By understanding this diverse range of treatment and intervention approaches, you can create characters whose journeys towards regaining their voice feel authentic and empowering. The next section will explore the importance of self-advocacy and emotional support in managing voice disorders.

Myth Debunking

Crafting believable characters requires understanding the nuances of human communication. Voice disorders can add depth and complexity to your characters, but these conditions are often shrouded in myths and stereotypes. Here's how to avoid perpetuating misconceptions when writing characters with voice disorders.

- **Myth: Voice disorders equal weakness or lack of confidence.**

This stereotype simply isn't true. Voice disorders can arise from various factors, and a character with a raspy voice or limited volume can still be strong and assertive. Don't conflate their vocal limitations with their personality traits.

- **Myth: Only singers and performers get voice disorders.**

While vocal strain can be a factor, voice disorders affect people from all walks of life. Explore the impact on a seasoned teacher with chronic hoarseness or a shy librarian struggling with vocal nodules. Consider how their disorder might influence their chosen profession or their interactions with others.

- **Myth: Voice disorders are temporary and always go away.**

While some voice disorders are temporary (like laryngitis), others can be chronic. Consider the challenges faced by a character who has lived with a voice disorder for years, impacting their ability to connect with loved ones or advocate for themselves. Explore their coping mechanisms and their moments of frustration.

- **Myth: Voice disorders are caused by misuse or bad habits.**

While vocal strain can worsen some disorders, many have underlying causes beyond a character's control. These can include neurological conditions, allergies, or even hormonal changes. Show the character's efforts to manage their voice, perhaps using alternative communication methods or seeking professional help.

- **Myth: People with voice disorders can't communicate effectively.**

This is a misconception. People with voice disorders often develop alternative strategies to get their message across. Give your character creative ways to express themselves, highlighting their resilience and resourcefulness. Perhaps they use technology like text-to-speech or rely heavily on facial expressions and gestures.

- **Myth: Voice disorders are a sign of emotional instability.**

There's no link between voice disorders and mental health. Explore a character with a voice disorder who is known for their calm demeanor and thoughtful communication style.

- **Myth: People with voice disorders should avoid social interaction.**

With proper treatment and vocal hygiene practices, individuals can manage their voice disorders and participate in social activities. Show a character overcoming their anxiety to engage in a conversation, proving that their voice, however different, deserves to be heard.

Remember:

By understanding and avoiding these myths, you can create characters with voice disorders who are well-rounded and relatable. Let your characters speak their truth, free from stereotypes. Their voice, whatever its form, can be a powerful tool for communication and self-expression.

Examples

Spasmodic dysphonia

The aroma of freshly brewed coffee filled the air as Sarah reached for the cafe door. Inside, a cozy buzz of conversation mingled with the rhythmic hiss of the espresso machine. She spotted her friend, David, hunched over a laptop at a corner table.

As she approached, Sarah noticed a faint furrow in his brow. "Hey, David," she greeted, her voice a touch lower than usual.

David looked up, a smile lighting up his face. "Sarah! Great to see you. Grab a seat, I'll just..." He trailed off, his brow furrowing further. He cleared his throat, a strained sound that seemed to catch in his throat.

Sarah settled into the chair opposite him, a flicker of concern crossing her features. "Everything okay, David?"

He nodded, a determined glint in his eyes. "Yeah, just... having a bit of a vocal hiccup this morning. Spasmodic dysphonia, you know the drill." A dry chuckle escaped his lips, but it was cut short by another strained cough.

Sarah offered a sympathetic smile. "Of course. Want me to order for you?"

"Actually," David said, his voice a breathy rasp, "I was practicing this new presentation for work. Trying to get the flow right, you see."

"A presentation, huh?" Sarah raised an eyebrow, intrigued. "What's it about?"

David took a deep breath, his voice returning to a near-normal level, though a hint of strain lingered. "It's about sustainable energy solutions. I've been working on some new ideas for reducing our company's carbon footprint."

"Sustainability, huh?" Sarah leaned forward, her eyes sparkling with interest. "You know, my sister's been really into that lately. Maybe you two could connect sometime."

David's face lit up. "That would be fantastic! But first," he said, a touch of self-consciousness creeping into his voice, "I need to get this presentation right. These vocal hiccups tend to throw me off a bit."

"Well," Sarah said, a mischievous glint in her eyes, "tell you what. How about we do a practice run? I can be the tough audience, and you can see if the ideas land even with a little... vocal interruption."

David chuckled, a genuine sound this time. "Sounds like a plan. Just don't expect award-winning acting from me."

Explanation for Writers:

- **Show, Don't Tell:** The narrative describes the strained quality of David's voice ("strained sound that seemed to catch in his throat") and his throat clearing without explicitly stating he has spasmodic dysphonia.
- **Context is Key:** The dialogue uses phrases like "vocal hiccup" and "these vocal hiccups tend to throw me off a bit" to provide context for David's speech patterns without dwelling on the technical term.
- **Focus on Character:** The dialogue focuses on David's ideas and personality, showcasing his passion for sustainability. His spasmodic dysphonia is a part of him, but it doesn't define him.

TEVP

Sarah stirred the caramel drizzle into her latte, watching the swirls dissolve into a milky haze. Across the table, John was deep in conversation about his new app, his voice a touch different than she remembered. It wasn't the booming baritone that could once fill a room, but a slightly raspy whisper that still held its familiar warmth.

John had undergone surgery a week ago, a cruel twist of fate silencing his vibrant voice. Now, a small, transparent disc rested on his neck, a tracheoesophageal voice prosthesis (TEVP) acting as a bridge between his lungs and his esophagus. It took Sarah a moment to get used to, this new way John spoke, a subtle difference that lingered on the edges of her perception.

"Hey, is everything alright?" she asked, noticing his shoulders hunch slightly as he spoke. "You seem a little winded."

John chuckled, a dry sound escaping his lips before the TEVP translated it into a breathy laugh. It wasn't quite the boisterous laugh she used to love, but the sound still warmed her heart. He discretely reached up and covered a small opening on his throat for a moment before speaking again.

"Yeah, just need to catch my breath. Talking can be tiring with this new setup."

Sarah reached across the table and squeezed his hand, her touch a silent reassurance. "Of course," she said softly. "Take your time. Maybe we can head outside for some fresh air?"

John smiled, a familiar glint returning to his eyes. "Sounds good. Besides, the barista keeps giving me weird looks when I cover my throat like a magician."

Sarah couldn't help but laugh, the sound echoing through the bustling coffee shop. "Right, let's avoid any unnecessary confusion."

They finished their drinks in companionable silence, the familiar rhythm of their relationship settling in despite the slight alteration. Stepping out into the cool afternoon air, John took a deep breath, his chest expanding fully.

"Isn't it amazing how much you take these simple things for granted?" he said, his voice slightly breathless but carrying a note of wonder.

Sarah looked at him, her heart swelling with a fierce love. John, always finding beauty in the everyday. "We'll get through this," she *said, her voice firm. "Together."*

He squeezed her hand back, his eyes crinkling at the corners. "To-gether. Always."

They walked along the tree-lined street, the golden light of the setting sun painting their path. The world hummed with the sounds of traffic and laughter, a symphony of life that John was now experiencing in a new way. He might not have his old voice, but the essence of who he was – his humor, his passion, his love – remained unchanged. And in that quiet truth, Sarah found a strength that echoed his own. They would navigate this new normal, side by side, their voices, both old and new, weaving a tapestry of love and resilience.

- **Natural Conversation:** Keep dialogue flowing, use TEVP as a background detail. Show its presence with brief actions (signals, covering stoma) and slight voice changes.
- **Character Reactions:TEVP user:** Acknowledge challenges with humor/frustration, express emotions naturally (vocally and non-verbally).
- **Others:** Be supportive and understanding.
- **TEVP as a Trait:** Part of the journey, not the definition. Focus on personality, goals, and relationships.

Giving Voice to the Voiceless: Portraying Characters with Voice Disorders

Imagine a character struggling to be heard, not because of the noise around them, but because of a condition affecting their very voice. Creating characters with voice disorders requires sensitivity, empathy, and a commitment to authenticity. This section equips you to craft characters whose journeys with vocal dysfunction feel real and relatable.

Beyond the Stereotypes: Building Authentic Characters

Authenticity is key. Research the specific characteristics of different voice disorders, like dysphonia or vocal fold paralysis. Consider consulting with individuals who have lived experiences with these conditions. This ensures your portrayal goes beyond stereotypes and captures the nuances of each character's struggles.

A Multifaceted Challenge: Exploring the Impact of Voice Disorders

Voice disorders aren't just about sounding different. They can impact a character's entire life – their ability to communicate, their self-esteem, and their social interactions. Explore the emotional and psychological aspects alongside the physical challenges. Show how your character grapples with their voice, not just how it sounds.

Struggles and Coping Mechanisms: With Empathy, Not Pity

Characters with voice disorders face frustration, embarrassment, and even isolation. Depict these struggles with sensitivity. Highlight their efforts to adapt, their coping mechanisms, and how they navigate everyday situations. Remember, empathy is key – show their struggles without resorting to pity.

Shattering Misconceptions: Redefining Strength

There's a misconception that voice disorders equal weakness. Challenge this stereotype! Show your character's inner strength and resilience. They face challenges head-on, finding ways to communicate and express themselves despite their vocal limitations.

Strength and Resilience: A Beacon of Hope

Characters with voice disorders are testaments to human resilience. By highlighting their determination to overcome obstacles, you inspire readers and foster empathy. Show how they find their voice, not just literally, but in their spirit and actions.

Empowering Characters: A Call to Action

Empowering characters with voice disorders goes beyond just creating them. It's about advocating for their rights, challenging stigma, and promoting understanding.

- **Advocacy and Support:** Show characters taking charge of their health. They seek professional help, join support groups, and become active participants in their own recovery.
- **Seeking Treatment and Resources:** Depict their journey towards seeking treatment and resources. This showcases their courage, determination, and the challenges they overcome on the path to vocal health.
- **Challenging Stigma:** Literature can dismantle stereotypes by portraying characters with dignity and complexity. This paves the way for acceptance and understanding.
- **Promoting Understanding and Inclusion:** Educate both characters and readers about voice disorders. Weave information about causes, symptoms, and treatments into your narrative. This empowers characters and readers with knowledge and fosters empathy.
- **Fostering Acceptance:** Ultimately, the goal is to create stories that celebrate the inherent value and dignity of all individuals, regardless of their communication methods. Through authentic representation and empathetic storytelling, you can inspire a world where everyone has a voice, and everyone is heard.

By following these guidelines, you can create characters with voice disorders who are not defined by their limitations, but who inspire readers with their strength, resilience, and the unwavering human spirit.

The Last Word: Empowering Voices Through Story

The final chapter isn't written yet. The journey towards inclusivity and understanding for individuals with voice disorders continues. As authors, we hold the power to shape that narrative, one story at a time.

Empowering characters with voice disorders isn't about creating a problem – it's about crafting a solution. By becoming advocates, educators, and storytellers who champion empathy and support, we can:

- **Champion Advocacy and Support:** Show characters taking charge of their health. They research resources, seek professional help, and connect with support groups. Let them be active participants in their own vocal recovery.
- **Educate Characters and Readers:** Weave knowledge into your narrative. Teach characters and readers about voice disorders, their causes, symptoms, and available treatments. Empowerment starts with understanding.
- **Challenge Stereotypes with Empathy:** Shatter misconceptions by portraying characters with dignity and complexity. Let their struggles be real, their strength undeniable. This paves the way for acceptance and understanding.
- **Amplify Diverse Voices:** Not everyone communicates the same way. Celebrate that! Through authentic representation, you give voice to the voiceless, fostering empathy for individuals with diverse communication needs.

Ultimately, our goal is to create stories that resonate with the inherent value and dignity of all people. Let's craft narratives where everyone has a voice, and everyone is heard. By embracing diversity, challenging stigma, and promoting empathy, we can enrich the literary landscape and create a world where true inclusion thrives.

So, the next time you develop a character, consider the power of a voice, not just in its volume, but in its resilience, its spirit, and its unwavering ability to be heard.

For Further Information:

- **American Speech-Language Hearing Association:** https://www.asha.org/practice-portal/clinical-topics/voice-disorders/
- **John Hopkins Medicine:** https://www.hopkinsmedicine.org/health/conditions-and-diseases/voice-disorders
- **Mayo Clinic**: https://www.mayoclinic.org/diseases-conditions/voice-disorders/symptoms-causes/syc-20353022
- **The 4 Underlying Causes of a Hoarse Voice (with examples)**:https://youtu.be/SwfrCKt1WaE?si=3xFYvCJL0-OHY1AS
- **After your Laryngectomy:** https://youtu.be/gwQ7MPjdmoo?si=MgeKbB749Vx5PAZJ
- **Statistics by the National Institute of Deafness and Other Communication Disorders:** https://www.nidcd.nih.gov/health/statistics/quick-statistics-voice-speech-language
- **Cancer Reasearch UK - Voice Prosthesis after Laryngectomy:** https://www.cancerresearchuk.org/about-cancer/laryngeal-cancer/living-with/speaking-after-laryngectomy/voice-prosthesis
- **National Health Service on Selective Mutism:** https://www.nhs.uk/mental-health/conditions/selective-mutism/
- **Selective Mutism Association:** https://www.selectivemutism.org/
- **American Speech-Language Hearing Association on Selective Mutism:** https://www.asha.org/public/speech/disorders/selective-mutism/

Character Checklist: Voice Disorders

This checklist is designed to help you develop a character with a voice disorder in a sensitive and authentic way.

Character Background:

- Specific Voice Disorder: What type of voice disorder does your character have? (e.g., Dysphonia, Aphonia, Vocal Fold Paralysis)
- Age of Onset: When did the voice disorder develop (childhood, adulthood)? Was there a triggering event (e.g., overuse, injury)?
- When were they diagnosed? Who diagnosed them? What was the professional's attitude toward the disorder? How did they feel about the diagnosis? Were they given advice/recommendations?
- Severity: How severe is the voice disorder? Does it cause hoarseness, breathiness, or complete voice loss?
- Cause (if known): Is there a known cause for the voice disorder (e.g., vocal nodules, medical condition)?

Speech Characteristics:

- Volume: Can your character speak at a normal volume, or is their voice weak or breathy?
- Pitch: Does your character's voice sound higher or lower than usual?
- Quality: Does your character's voice sound hoarse, raspy, or strained?
- Speech Intelligibility: Is your character's speech easily understood, or is it difficult to hear them clearly?

Communication Strategies:

- Self-Monitoring: Is your character aware of their voice problems? Do they try to conserve their voice or avoid certain speaking situations?
- Alternative Communication: Does your character use alternative com-

munication methods (e.g., writing, assistive devices) to supplement speech?

- Medical Treatment: Has your character received medical treatment (e.g., vocal rest, voice therapy) for their voice disorder?
- What strategy do they use when communication fails? How do they react?

Emotional Impact:

- Frustration: Does your character experience frustration due to their voice limitations?
- Isolation: Does the voice disorder lead to social isolation or difficulty making themselves heard?
- Confidence: How does the voice disorder impact your character's self-confidence and ability to communicate effectively?
- Self-Consciousness: Does your character feel self-conscious about their voice and avoid speaking in public?

Additional Considerations:

- Impact on Profession: Does the voice disorder affect your character's choice of profession or ability to perform their job duties?
- Support System: Does your character have a supportive family, friends, or colleagues who understand their voice disorder?
- Character Development: How does the voice disorder shape your character's personality, coping mechanisms, and communication strategies?

Narrative Choices:

- Dialogue: How will you represent your character's voice disorder in writing (descriptive language, variations in punctuation)?
- Internal Monologue: Will you use internal monologue to explore your character's thoughts and anxieties about their voice?

- Balance: Have you balanced authenticity with the need for clear and engaging storytelling?

Character Development:

- Strengths and Struggles: How does your character's voice disorder impact their daily life and interactions with others?
- Beyond Speech: What are your character's strengths and personality traits beyond their voice disorder?
- Avoid Stereotypes: Have you avoided relying solely on their voice disorder to define your character?

Representation:

- Respectful Portrayal: Have you portrayed your character's voice disorder with respect and sensitivity?
- Avoidance of Caricatures: Have you avoided stereotypical or exaggerated representations of people with voice disorders?
- Inclusion of options: Have you given your character options for treatment and coping?

Remember:

- This checklist is a starting point; not all characters with voice disorders will experience all of these aspects.
- Research the specific voice disorder to ensure an accurate portrayal.
- Consider including resources for readers who want to learn more.
- Focus on your character's unique voice (beyond the physical limitations), resilience, and alternative communication methods.

Challenge Accepted: Experiencing Vocal Strain for a Day to Deepen Your Characters

Crafting characters with voice disorders requires a nuanced understanding of the challenges they face. Research is key, but to truly connect with their struggles, consider this bold proposition: **try experiencing vocal strain for a day.**

What is Vocal Strain?

Vocal strain occurs when the vocal cords are overworked or misused. This can lead to hoarseness, vocal fatigue, and even pain when speaking.

The Challenge: 24 Hours of Vocal Discomfort

For 24 hours, consciously modify your vocal habits to simulate the experience of vocal strain. Here are some ways to achieve this:

- **Whispering:** Speak in a whisper for most of the day. This reduces vocal fold vibration, mimicking the feeling of a hoarse voice.
- **Limited Volume:** Avoid raising your voice above a soft conversational level.
- **Forced Pitch:** Speak in a higher or lower pitch than your natural speaking voice, creating additional strain on your vocal cords.
- **Limited Talking:** Minimize unnecessary conversation throughout the day.

Why Experience Vocal Strain?

- **Empathy Through Experience:** This isn't about mimicking a specific disorder. It's about understanding the physical discomfort and communication limitations associated with vocal strain.
- **Beyond Raspy Voices:** Vocal strain manifests in different ways. This

challenge broadens your perspective on how it can impact a character's communication.

- **Respectful Representation:** By experiencing the frustrations of vocal strain, you gain a deeper appreciation for the resilience and communication strategies people with voice disorders develop.

Important Considerations:

- **Safety:** If you have any pre-existing vocal issues, consult a doctor or voice therapist before attempting this challenge. Stop if you experience any pain or discomfort.
- **Communication Alternatives:** Explore alternative communication methods like writing, texting, or sign language to compensate for limited speaking.
- **Focus on Intent:** While your voice may be limited, remember to focus on getting your message across effectively.

The Power of Vulnerability

This challenge isn't about replicating a medical condition perfectly. It's about opening yourself up to a new experience. By experiencing the limitations of vocal strain, even for a day, you'll gain a deeper understanding of the characters you create. This empathy will translate into richer, more authentic portrayals, ensuring your characters with voice disorders are not defined by their limitations, but by their strength and determination.

Are you ready to accept the challenge?

7

Language Disorders

The Untold Story: Understanding Language Disorders in Characters

H ave you ever considered the silent struggle of a character who can't quite grasp what others are saying, or who finds expressing themselves a frustrating hurdle? Language disorders affect millions of people worldwide, and yet, their experiences are often invisible in storytelling.

This section dives deep into the complexities of language disorders, equipping you to craft characters whose struggles and triumphs with communication feel real and relatable. By understanding the nature and impact of these conditions, you can create characters who are not defined by their limitations, but who inspire with their resilience and perseverance.

Beyond the Stumble: What are Language Disorders?

Language disorders are more than just mispronouncing words or getting grammar wrong. They encompass a range of challenges that hinder an individual's ability to understand and use language effectively. Imagine a character struggling to put their thoughts into words, or constantly missing the punchline of a joke – these are just some of the ways language disorders can manifest.

A Spectrum of Difficulties: Receptive vs. Expressive

Language disorders can affect how a character receives and interprets information, or how they express themselves. Think of it like two sides of the communication coin:

- **Receptive Language:** Does your character have trouble understanding spoken instructions or following a story? They might have a receptive language disorder, making it difficult to grasp the meaning of what others are saying.
- **Expressive Language:** Perhaps your character struggles to form sentences or express their ideas clearly. This could be a sign of an expressive language disorder, where putting thoughts into words becomes a constant battle.

The Building Blocks of Language:

Language is a complex system with different components that work together. Understanding how these building blocks can be affected by language disorders is crucial:

- **Syntax:** Imagine the grammar rules that hold a sentence together. Syntax difficulties can make it hard for characters to structure their sentences correctly.
- **Semantics:** This is all about word meaning. Characters with semantic problems might struggle to understand the meaning of certain words or phrases, leading to confusion and misunderstandings.
- **Morphology:** Ever wonder how words are formed? Morphology deals with prefixes, suffixes, and word roots. Difficulties in this area can make

it challenging to break down complex words or create new ones.

- **Pragmatics:** This is where language meets social situations. Pragmatic challenges can make it difficult for characters to understand the unspoken rules of communication, like taking turns in conversation or using appropriate language in different settings.

Supralinguistics: The Unspoken Language of Critical Thinking:

Supralinguistics isn't just about fancy jargon – it's the secret sauce that makes communication truly rich and nuanced. Imagine it as the missing piece of the puzzle, the hidden layer of meaning that goes beyond the spoken word.

Here, nonverbal cues, body language, and cultural references all come together to create a symphony of understanding. But for characters with supralinguistic difficulties, this symphony becomes a cacophony – they struggle to decipher the unspoken language that fuels critical thinking, problem-solving, humor, and even understanding double meanings.

Critical Thinking and Problem-Solving: Beyond the Obvious

Supralinguistics is a key component of critical thinking, the ability to analyze information, evaluate arguments, and draw sound conclusions.

Think of a character who takes everything at face value. They might miss the sarcasm in a friend's comment or struggle to understand the underlying message in a political cartoon.

Supralinguistic difficulties can make it challenging to "read between the lines" and grasp the full context of a situation, hindering critical thinking and problem-solving skills.

The Humor Factor: When Jokes Fall Flat

Humor thrives on surprise and the ability to understand layers of meaning. Imagine a character who misses the playful wink in a friend's teasing or takes a sarcastic remark literally.

Supralinguistic challenges can make it difficult to appreciate humor, leading to social awkwardness and a sense of being left out. By portraying characters who struggle with humor due to supralinguistic difficulties, you can explore the complexities of social interaction and the importance of understanding the "unspoken language" of jokes and lighthearted banter.

Double Trouble: Decoding Hidden Meanings

Double meanings are like puzzles within words, where one phrase can have two interpretations. Imagine a character who interprets a compliment as an insult because they miss the nonverbal cues or cultural context that convey the speaker's true intent.

Supralinguistic difficulties can make it challenging to decode double meanings or make inferences,leading to misunderstandings and misinterpretations. This can have a significant impact on a character's social interactions and emotional well-being.

By incorporating supralinguistic challenges into your characters, you can create a deeper understanding of the complexities of communication. These characters won't just struggle to understand spoken words – they'll grapple with the entire ecosystem of nonverbal cues, cultural references, and unspoken messages that make communication truly meaningful.

This can add a layer of realism and complexity to your characters, making them even more relatable and engaging for your readers.

The Ripple Effect: Impact on Everyday Life

Language disorders aren't just frustrating – they can have a significant impact on a character's life. Imagine the challenges of navigating school when understanding lectures is difficult, or feeling isolated because you can't quite connect with others. This section will delve deeper into the social, academic, and emotional consequences of language disorders, equipping you to create characters whose struggles resonate with your readers.

Please note:

The information presented in this book is intended to provide writers with a general understanding of communication disorders. It is not a replacement for a professional evaluation by a qualified Speech-Language Pathologist (SLP). If you suspect someone may have a communication disorder, please consult with an SLP for diagnosis and treatment recommendations.

Types of Language Disorders

Language disorders affect millions of people worldwide, impacting their ability to communicate and interact with others. As an author, understanding these conditions allows you to create characters who feel real and relatable, even when their experiences with language differ from your own.

This section dives into the various types of language disorders, equipping you to craft characters whose struggles and triumphs with communication resonate with your readers.

Aphasia: When a Stroke Takes Your Words

Imagine a character who suddenly struggles to find the right words, or who can understand perfectly yet can't form a complete sentence.

Aphasia, often caused by stroke or brain injury, disrupts the connection between the brain and language. Here, we explore different subtypes of aphasia:

- **Broca's Aphasia:** Frustration boils over as your character tries to speak, their thoughts trapped behind a jumble of broken phrases. Broca's aphasia affects speech production, making it difficult to form grammatically correct sentences. While comprehension may remain intact, expressing themselves becomes a constant battle. They may speak in telegraphic, incomplete sentences.

- **Wernicke's Aphasia:** The world around your character becomes a confusing mix of sounds. Wernicke's aphasia affects comprehension, making it hard to understand spoken language or written text. Speech may flow easily, but it often lacks meaning or coherence. This nonsensical speech may be referred to as "word salad."
- **Global Aphasia:** Imagine the silence that follows a devastating blow. Global aphasia is the most severe form, impacting both comprehension and speech production. Communication becomes an immense challenge, requiring alternative methods to bridge the gap.

Beyond Aphasia: Other Language Disorders

The landscape of language disorders extends beyond aphasia:

- **Alzheimer's and Dementia:** As degenerative diseases ravage the brain, language can become a casualty. Your characters might struggle to find words, their sentences growing fragmented as the disease progresses.
- **Dyslexia:** The written word becomes a puzzle. Characters with dyslexia might wrestle with reading fluency, misspelling words, or struggling to decode written text.

Developmental Language Disorders: When Language Doesn't Follow the Expected Path

Language acquisition is a wondrous journey, but for some children, this path takes unexpected turns. Developmental language disorders encompass a range of conditions that affect how children learn and use language.

Understanding the Difference: A slight delay in babbling or forming first words might be a normal variation in development. However, a persistent struggle to comprehend language or express oneself could indicate a language disorder.

Communication Milestones as a Guide:

Imagine a roadmap for language development. Understanding these milestones, from early babbling to complex sentence structures, equips you to create characters whose communication skills reflect their age and stage of development.

A toddler struggling to follow simple instructions or a teenager who speaks in short, grammatically incorrect sentences – these details can add depth and authenticity to your characters.

By exploring the complexities of language disorders, you gain the power to create a wider spectrum of characters, each with their unique voice and communication style. Remember, true storytelling isn't just about what is said, but also about the beauty of overcoming challenges to find a way to connect and be heard.

Why Words Sometimes Get Lost: Causes of Language Disorders

Language disorders can stem from a variety of factors, making it a complex puzzle for both characters and the people who create them. This section dives into the underlying causes and contributing elements, equipping you to craft characters whose struggles with communication feel authentic.

Brain Glitches: When Neurology Disrupts Language

Sometimes, the very machinery of communication malfunctions. Language disorders can arise due to neurological factors like:

- **Brain Injury:** A sudden blow to the head can disrupt the intricate dance of neurons responsible for language processing. This can lead to difficulties with comprehension or expression, depending on the specific area of the brain affected.

- **Stroke:** Imagine a vital pathway blocked, cutting off communication between brain regions. Strokes can damage areas crucial for language function, resulting in aphasia or other language deficits.
- **Neurodevelopmental Disorders:** Conditions like autism spectrum disorder can affect brain development in ways that impact language skills. These disorders might cause delays or atypical patterns in language acquisition.

The Brain's Language Map: Where Words Are Made

The brain is a magnificent control center, and language processing has its own dedicated corner. Understanding these regions is key to comprehending language disorders:

- **Broca's Area:** Located in the left hemisphere, damage to Broca's area can lead to Broca's aphasia, making it difficult to form fluent sentences.
- **Wernicke's Area:** Conversely, Wernicke's aphasia arises from damage to Wernicke's area, causing challenges in understanding spoken language.
- **Frontal Lobe:** The planning center of the brain, can cause issues with pragmatics and supralinguistics.

Picture these as the headquarters for speech production and comprehension, respectively. There are many other areas that assist with speech and language, such as the angular gyrus, the primary auditory cortex, and the white matter tract.

Beyond the Brain: Genes and Environment

The story doesn't end with the brain. Language disorders can also have:

- **Genetic Components:** Certain conditions like Down syndrome have a genetic basis, increasing the likelihood of developing language difficulties.

- **Environmental Influences:** The environment plays a crucial role in shaping language skills. Exposure to rich language, quality early care-giving, and educational opportunities all contribute to strong language development.
- **Socio-economic factors and cultural differences:** can influence language acquisition and sometimes contribute to language disorders.

By understanding the complex interplay of neurological, genetic, and environmental factors, you can create characters whose language struggles feel real and grounded in the complexities of human development. Remember, communication is a journey, and sometimes the path takes unexpected turns.

The Ripple Effect: How Language Disorders Impact Lives

Language disorders are more than just stumbling over words or getting grammar wrong. They can create a ripple effect throughout a character's life, impacting everything from social interactions to academic success.

Understanding these manifestations and their impact is crucial for crafting characters who feel authentic and relatable.

The Struggles to Speak and Understand: A Spectrum of Symptoms

Imagine a character struggling to find the right words, or constantly missing the punchline of a joke. These are just some of the ways language disorders can manifest:

- **Speech Production:** Putting thoughts into words can be a constant battle. Characters with speech production difficulties might stammer, speak in short phrases, or struggle to articulate their ideas clearly.
- **Comprehension:** The world around them becomes a confusing puzzle.

Characters with comprehension difficulties might miss instructions, misunderstand jokes, or have trouble following conversations.

- **Vocabulary and Grammar:** The building blocks of language can become stumbling points. Characters might struggle to find the right words, misuse grammar, or have difficulty constructing sentences.

It's Not One-Size-Fits-All: A Range of Severity

The good news? Language disorders affect everyone differently. Some characters might experience mild symptoms, occasionally stumbling over a word or two. Others might face more profound challenges, significantly impacting their ability to communicate. Remember, it's a spectrum, and your characters can exist anywhere along it.

Beyond Words: Social and Academic Impact

The impact of language disorders goes beyond spoken communication:

- **Social Struggles:** Making friends or engaging in casual conversation can feel like climbing a mountain. Characters with language disorders might struggle to connect with others, leading to feelings of isolation and loneliness.
- **Academic Challenges:** School can become a minefield of frustration. Difficulties with reading, writing, and comprehension can hinder learning and academic achievement.
- **Behavioral Challenges:** Sometimes, frustration boils over. The challenges of communication can lead to behavioral outbursts or social withdrawal as characters struggle to express themselves effectively.

The Emotional Toll: Self-Esteem and Identity

Language disorders aren't just about communication – they can impact a character's entire sense of self:

- Bruised Self-Esteem: Constantly struggling to be understood can take a toll on confidence. Characters might develop feelings of inadequacy or embarrassment due to their communication difficulties.
- Shaken Identity: Language is a core part of who we are. Characters with language disorders might grapple with their sense of identity, questioning how their communication challenges define them.
- Anxiety and Depression: The weight of communication struggles can be heavy. Characters might experience anxiety, frustration, or even depression due to the challenges they face.

Beyond the Words on the Page: Creating Empathy

By understanding the impact of language disorders, you can create characters who feel real and relatable. Remember, these challenges don't define who they are.

They are individuals with stories to tell, dreams to chase, and the strength to overcome obstacles. Let their struggles inspire empathy and understanding, reminding us all of the beauty of communication, in all its diverse forms.

Behind the Curtain: Unveiling the Diagnosis of Language Disorders

Creating a character with a language disorder requires stepping into the shoes of a detective – piecing together the puzzle to understand their unique communication challenges.

This section equips you with the knowledge of how language disorders are assessed and diagnosed, allowing you to craft authentic and realistic portrayals.

The Evaluation Journey: Unveiling the Language Puzzle

Imagine a character struggling to communicate. To understand why, we embark on an evaluation process, typically led by a speech-language pathologist (SLP). Here's a glimpse into what this journey entails:

The SLP's Toolkit: Unveiling Language Skills

The SLP has a toolbox filled with assessment tools to pinpoint the specific language difficulties:

- **Gathering Clues: Medical History and Development** Just like any good detective, the SLP gathers information. They'll delve into the character's medical history, developmental milestones, and current communication skills through interviews, observations, and standardized assessments.
- **Standardized Tests:** Imagine a language IQ test. Standardized tests like CELF or TOLD provide a snapshot of a character's vocabulary, grammar, and overall language skills.
- **Language Samples:** These are like eavesdropping on a conversation. The SLP interacts with the character, collecting a sample of their natural speech. This allows them to see how they use language in everyday situations, beyond the pressures of a formal test.

- **Informal Observations:** Sometimes, the most revealing clues lie in everyday interactions. The SLP might observe how the character understands instructions, participates in conversations, or uses gestures to communicate.

Decoding the Language Sample: From Recording to Analysis
Once the SLP has a language sample, the detective work truly begins:

- **Transcription:** The recording is transformed into written text, capturing every word, pause, and even nonverbal cues like gestures.
- **Analysis:** Imagine examining a fingerprint. The SLP analyzes the transcribed sample, looking at vocabulary usage, sentence structure, word meaning, and how effectively the character communicates.
- **Quantitative and Qualitative Measures:** There's a blend of science and detective intuition here. The SLP might calculate sentence length or analyze the types of errors made, while also observing how the character uses communication strategies to overcome challenges.

Collaboration is Key: Working with a Team of Specialists

No detective works alone. The SLP often collaborates with other professionals:

- **Neuropsychologists:** These specialists can provide insights into the cognitive and neurological aspects of language, helping to paint a more complete picture.
- **Audiologists:** These specialists perform hearing and vestibular testing.

Ruling Out Other Suspects: Differential Diagnosis

Sometimes, similar symptoms can have different causes. Differential diagnosis involves distinguishing language disorders from other conditions like intellectual disabilities or learning disabilities. A thorough assessment ensures an accurate diagnosis and the most effective intervention.

Co-existing Conditions: A Multifaceted Challenge

Language disorders can sometimes team up with other conditions like ADHD. Identifying these co-occurring challenges is crucial for creating a comprehensive intervention plan.

Language Disorder vs. Language Difference: Knowing the Difference

It's important to remember that not every difference in communication is a disorder. While a language disorder significantly impacts a character's ability to communicate and learn, a language difference simply reflects variations in language use due to cultural background or regional dialect.

By understanding the assessment and diagnosis process, you can create characters whose language challenges feel real and believable. Remember, a diagnosis is just the beginning of the story. These characters have strengths, dreams, and the resilience to overcome communication hurdles.

Building Bridges: Treatment and Intervention for Language Disorders

The world can feel like a confusing puzzle for characters with language disorders. But there's hope! This section dives into the various treatment and intervention approaches that can equip them with the tools they need to bridge the communication gap.

The SLP's Toolkit: Techniques to Unlock Language

Speech-language pathologists (SLPs) are the communication detectives, armed with a variety of techniques to target specific challenges:

- **Structured Activities:** Imagine a language gym. Structured activities like word games and storytelling exercises help characters strengthen vocabulary, grammar, and comprehension skills in a fun and engaging way.
- **Language Stimulation:** Surround your characters with a language buffet! Language stimulation involves exposing them to rich conversations, books, pictures, and multimedia resources – the more language they encounter, the more they'll learn.
- **Semantic Mapping:** Think of it as a mind map for words. Semantic mapping helps characters organize their vocabulary by connecting new words to familiar ones, making learning and remembering easier.
- **Narrative Intervention:** Unleash the inner storyteller! Narrative intervention helps characters develop storytelling skills, improve sequencing, and boost their ability to understand the hidden meaning behind stories.
- **Visual Supports:** A picture is worth a thousand words, especially for characters struggling with language. Visual schedules, picture cards, and communication boards provide essential visual cues to support understanding and expression.
- **AAC Strategies:** For characters with severe communication difficulties, Augmentative and Alternative Communication (AAC) steps in. This might involve using communication devices, symbol systems, or even sign language to help them express themselves and understand others.
- **Play-Based Therapy:** Learning through play? Absolutely! Play-based therapy uses games and imaginative scenarios to target language goals in a fun and engaging way, fostering social interaction and motivation.

Remember: These techniques are like building blocks, customized to fit each character's unique needs. Through consistent practice and targeted intervention, they can develop their communication skills and navigate the world with greater confidence.

A Team Effort: Collaboration is Key

No single approach works in isolation. Effective intervention often involves a team effort from Educators, Occupational Therapists, Behavioral Specialists. Educators ensure language interventions are integrated into the classroom, while occupational therapists and behavioral specialists might address underlying sensory or behavioral factors that impact communication.

Family Matters: The Power of Support

The people closest to your characters play a vital role in their journey. Family-centered intervention emphasizes collaboration between therapists and families. By working together, they can ensure communication strategies are seamlessly integrated into daily routines and activities, creating a supportive environment for language development.

By understanding the treatment and intervention landscape, you can create characters with language disorders who are not defined by their challenges, but empowered by their resilience and the support system around them.

Remember, communication is a journey, and with the right tools and support, even the most daunting obstacles can be overcome.

Debunking the Myths: Common Misconceptions About Language Disorders

Language disorders affect a person's ability to understand or express language. These can be complex conditions, and unfortunately, there are many myths and misunderstandings surrounding them. Here, we explore some of the most common myths to create a clearer picture:

- **Myth: Language disorders mean lower intelligence.**

Reality: Language disorders affect how someone communicates, not how they think. A person who struggles to express themselves verbally can be highly intelligent and have rich inner thoughts and ideas.

- **Myth: A developmental language disorder means a child has autism.**

Reality: While late talking can be a sign of a developmental delay, it's important to remember that many children with typical development simply hit language milestones at their own pace.

- **Myth: People with language disorders are lazy or don't try hard enough.**

Reality: Language disorders are not a choice. They can be caused by neurological factors, developmental delays, or even physical limitations. These individuals often put in a tremendous amount of effort to communicate effectively.

- **Myth: Language disorders are temporary and everyone outgrows them.**

Reality: While some language disorders improve with therapy or over time, others are chronic. Early intervention is crucial, but some individuals may require ongoing support throughout their lives.

· **Myth: People with language disorders can't communicate effectively.**

Reality: They often develop alternative communication strategies. These can include:

· Technology: Speech-generating devices or communication apps.
· Writing: Expressing themselves more effectively through written communication.
· Body Language: Relying on gestures and facial expressions to convey meaning.
· Drawing or AAC Systems: Utilizing Sign Language, picture boards or other Augmentative and Alternative Communication methods.
· **Myth: Language disorders only affect speaking.**

Reality: They can sometimes impact reading, writing, and spelling as well. A person may struggle with understanding written language or have difficulty putting their thoughts into words on paper.

· **Myth: Language disorders are "contagious" and can be "caught" by others.**

Reality: Language disorders are not infectious. They arise from specific underlying conditions, not imitation.

· **Myth: Telling someone to "slow down" or "take a deep breath" is helpful.**

Reality: While relaxation techniques can be part of therapy, unsolicited advice can be counterproductive. The focus should be on communication strategies that work for the individual.

· **Myth: All language disorders involve grammar.**

Reality: Grammar issues are just one aspect of language disorders. Others include difficulty finding words, problems with social skills, and challenges with understanding spoken language.

- **Myth: People with language disorders are more likely to experience anxiety or depression.**

Reality: There's no direct causal link. However, the social challenges associated with language disorders can contribute to anxiety or low self-esteem.

- **Myth: A language disorder means a person can never have a successful career.**

Reality: Many individuals with language disorders thrive in a variety of professions. With support and effective communication strategies, they can achieve their goals.

- **Myth: Children who talk late are automatically diagnosed with a language disorder.**

Reality: While delayed speech can be a sign of a language disorder, it's not always the case. Many children simply develop language skills at their own pace. Monitoring a child's overall language development patterns and consulting a professional if concerns arise is crucial.

- **Myth: Language disorders only affect children.**

Reality: Language disorders can occur at any age. Adults can experience aphasia due to stroke or brain injury, or develop specific language difficulties later in life.

- **Myth: Overcoming a language disorder means "fixing" the person.**

Reality: The focus should be on empowering communication. Language therapy and strategies aim to equip individuals with the tools they need to express themselves effectively, celebrating their unique communication styles.

- **Myth: People with language disorders are not good at foreign languages.**

Reality: Language learning can be challenging for anyone, including individuals with language disorders. However, with the right approach and support, they can still achieve success in learning another language.

- **Myth: Technology can "cure" language disorders.**

Reality: Technology like speech-generating devices or communication apps can be valuable tools for people with language disorders. However, they are not a replacement for therapy or strategies that address the underlying challenges.

By understanding these additional myths, we can promote a more informed and empathetic perspective on language disorders.

Examples

Wernicke's Aphasia

The hospital waiting room buzzed with a symphony of fluorescent lights and anxious coughs. Sarah drummed her fingers on the armrest, her worry growing with each passing minute. Her father, a man known for his witty stories and booming laughter, had been strangely quiet lately. Now, after a battery of tests, the doctor's words echoed in her mind: Wernicke's aphasia.

The door creaked open, and her father emerged, a lost look in his eyes. He shuffled towards her, a jumble of words tumbling from his lips like mismatched puzzle pieces.

"Sarah...clouds...butterflies...time traveling...clocks ticking..." he said, his voice unusually rapid and laced with a manic edge.

Sarah forced a smile, her heart clenching. "Hi Dad. How are you feeling?"

He frowned, frustration flickering across his face. "Feeling...purple elephants...teacups full of memories...need...need...need the winning lottery numbers!"

Sarah gently took his hand. "Let's sit down, okay? We can talk later."

He calmed slightly, his gaze flitting around the room. "Later...later... when the green monkeys sing opera...oh, there's the Queen hiding behind the potted fern!"

Despite the jumble of nonsensical words, Sarah felt a flicker of her father's usual humor in the nonsensical imagery. She decided to play along.

"Really, Dad? The Queen? Where?" she asked, peering behind the fern with a mock look of surprise.

A mischievous glint returned to his eyes. "Shhh! Don't scare her away! She's here on a secret mission...to steal all the hospital pudding!"

Sarah couldn't help but laugh, the sound echoing through the sterile room. It wasn't a normal conversation, but in that shared laughter, a connection sparked. The road ahead might be filled with challenges, but Sarah knew she wouldn't face them alone. Together, they would navigate this new reality, one nonsensical word salad at a time.

Key points for writers:

- Focus on rapid, tangential speech: Characters with Wernicke's aphasia may speak fluently, but their words may not be relevant or connected.
- Incorporate neologisms: They may invent new words or phrases that are nonsensical.
- Maintain a supportive tone: The character may become frustrated, so

patience and understanding are crucial.

· Look for underlying emotions: Though the words may be jumbled, the character may still be trying to express emotions like fear, frustration, or even humor.

Broca's Aphasia

The afternoon sun cast long shadows across the park bench as Sarah sat beside her grandmother, Helen. Helen, once a vibrant storyteller, now struggled to find the words she desperately wanted to express. Wernicke's aphasia, a cruel twist of fate, had snatched away her fluency, leaving behind a frustrating jumble of sounds and emotions.

Sarah squeezed Helen's hand, a silent reassurance in the face of her grandmother's growing frustration. Helen, her brow furrowed in concentration, pointed towards a group of children playing on the swings.

"They...happy..." Helen's voice trailed off, the word she searched for slipping through her grasp.

Sarah smiled, piecing together her grandmother's meaning. "Yes, the children seem happy. They're having so much fun swinging."

Helen nodded eagerly, a flicker of relief crossing her face. She reached into her purse and pulled out a crumpled photograph, her fingers tracing the faded image of a younger Sarah perched on a swing set.

"You...swing..." Helen began, her voice filled with a yearning Sarah understood all too well.

"Yes, Grandma," Sarah replied gently, taking the photo. "We used to swing together all the time. Remember how you used to push me so high?"

Helen's eyes lit up with a sudden spark of recognition. "High...fly..." she exclaimed, a triumphant smile breaking through her confusion.

Sarah chuckled, her heart swelling with bittersweet joy. "Yes, you used to say I flew like a bird."

They sat in comfortable silence for a moment, the photo acting as a

bridge between past and present. Sarah knew frustration and moments
of lucidity would continue to dance a complex waltz in Helen's mind.
Yet, in these brief exchanges, a deeper level of communication bloomed
– a communication built on patience, shared memories, and a love that
transcended the limitations of language.

Key points for writers:

- **Focus on non-verbal cues:** Use facial expressions, gestures, and objects (like the photo) to aid communication.
- **Maintain a positive and patient tone:** Characters with Wernicke's aphasia can become frustrated. Acknowledge their feelings, but maintain a calm and encouraging demeanor.
- **Focus on shared meaning:** Don't dwell on the missing words. Help the character express themselves through any available means, and celebrate moments of understanding.

Developmental language:

Here are some tips on how to write natural dialogue of a child with developmental language delays:

- **Focus on Meaning, Not Perfection:**
- **Prioritize understanding the child's intent** over grammatically perfect sentences.
- **Let the child's personality shine through** despite errors in syntax and morphology.
- **Incorporate Language Delays:**
- **Use simple sentence structures** with short phrases and limited clauses.
- **Incorporate word order errors:**Subject-verb agreement mistakes (e.g., "She goed outside" instead of "She went outside").
- Missing articles (e.g., "Want juice" instead of "I want juice").
- **Incorporate morphological errors:**Incorrect verb tenses (e.g., "Runned"

instead of "ran").

- Misuse of plurals (e.g., "Mouses" instead of "mice").
- Neologisms (invented words) that make sense in the child's context.
- **Maintain a Supportive Environment:**
- **Characters who interact with the child should be patient and encouraging.**
- **Adults can rephrase the child's words for clarity** without directly correcting them (e.g., "So you want a snack?" after the child says "Hungry!").
- **Use familiar references** and connect new concepts to things the child already understands.

Scenario: A child named Ben (age 4) wants to play with his toy car.

- **Unnatural Dialogue:** "Mommy, can I please play with the red car which is located on the top shelf?" (This is grammatically correct but sounds too formal for a young child.)
- **Natural Dialogue:** (Pointing) "Car! Up there! Play?" **Mother:** (Smiling) "You want to play with the red car? It is on the high shelf, isn't it? Let me help you get it."

Scenario: A child named Sarah (age 7) is describing her favorite cartoon.

- **Unnatural Dialogue:** "The purple monster chased the green superhero character around the entire city with great speed." (This is grammatically correct but lacks the enthusiasm children often display.)
- **Natural Dialogue:** "Purple monster! Big and mean! He chased Green Guy sooo fast! All around the city! Green Guy gotta zoom away!"

Remember:

- The severity of the language delays will vary by character.
- Observe real children with similar delays to capture their speech patterns

authentically.

- Focus on the emotional core of the conversation, not just the grammatical accuracy.

Giving Voice to the Unspoken: Portraying Characters with Language Disorders

Characters with language disorders deserve to be seen and heard, not defined by their limitations. This section equips you, the author, to craft authentic portrayals that capture the complexities of their experiences.

Creating Characters Who Ring True: Authenticity is Key

Before you write, do your research! Understand the specific language disorder your character has. Talk to people with similar conditions or consult with professionals. Authenticity builds bridges of empathy between readers and your characters.

Beyond Stumbling Words: The Nuances of Language Difficulties

Language disorders are a spectrum, not a one-size-fits-all situation.

Show the unique challenges your character faces – expressing themselves, understanding others, navigating social interactions. Highlight their frustrations, isolation, and the communication barriers they encounter. But don't forget their strengths and unique abilities!

Coping Mechanisms and Communication Strategies: A Balancing Act

Explore how your character copes with their language difficulties. Do they use creative workarounds? Rely on assistive technology? Seek support from loved ones? Be mindful of the emotional toll these challenges take on self-esteem, relationships, and quality of life. Show how they navigate everyday situations and strive to be understood, despite the obstacles.

Respectful Representation: Avoiding Stereotypes and Misconceptions

There's a misconception that language disorders mean someone is unintelligent. Challenge that! Instead, emphasize your character's intelligence, creativity, and resilience. Show the diversity within this community and avoid generalizations.

Inner Strength and Resilience: The Power Within

Your character's journey is about overcoming challenges. Highlight their determination, resourcefulness, and growth as they navigate communication difficulties. Celebrate their triumphs! Portray them as multifaceted individuals with hopes, dreams, and aspirations that go beyond their language disorder.

Empowering Characters with Language Disorders: Beyond the Challenges

Advocacy and Support: Taking Charge

Empower your character to be their own advocate. Show them seeking out speech therapy, assistive technology, and support groups. This normalizes seeking help and encourages readers to do the same.

Breaking Barriers: Challenging Stigma Through Representation

Language disorders shouldn't be a source of shame. Use your story to challenge misconceptions. Show how capable and intelligent your character is, despite the challenges they face. Portray them overcoming societal barriers and achieving their dreams.

Building Bridges of Understanding: Inclusion Matters

Showcase a diverse cast of characters with varying communication needs and abilities. Promote understanding of different communication styles and the importance of inclusive environments where everyone has a voice. Encourage empathy and acceptance by highlighting the shared humanity of all characters.

Educating Characters and Readers: Knowledge is Power

Weave accurate information about language disorders into your narrative. Explain different types, their causes, and impact on daily life. Let your characters learn from each other and grow in their understanding of diverse communication needs.

Fostering Empathy and Acceptance: The Heart of the Story

Show the emotional journey of your character – the highs and lows, triumphs and setbacks, the everyday joys and challenges. Help readers connect with the character's humanity, recognizing their worth and potential beyond their communication style.

By creating empowered characters with language disorders, you can break down stereotypes, foster understanding, and celebrate the beauty of communication in all its diverse forms.

The Final Chapter: Celebrating the Power of Words, Despite the Challenges

We've embarked on a journey to understand language disorders – the stumbles, the misunderstandings, the impact they have on people's lives. We've explored different disorders, from aphasia to dyslexia, and how they can affect communication, learning, and social interaction.

But this isn't just about the challenges. It's about the characters we bring to life. As authors, we have the power to shape how readers see the world. And when it comes to language disorders, authentic representation is key.

Characters with Dignity, Respect, and Authenticity

Imagine a character struggling to find the right words, or a student frustrated by the written word. By portraying these experiences with sensitivity, accuracy, and empathy, we can bridge the gap between readers and those with language disorders. We can show the challenges, yes, but also the strengths, the resilience, the unique way each character navigates the world.

Beyond the Page: Promoting Understanding and Inclusion

The written word has the power to transform. By embracing diversity in our characters, we can foster empathy and understanding in our readers. We can challenge stereotypes, celebrate the beauty of communication in all its forms, and inspire readers to become advocates for those with language disorders.

This is a call to action, fellow authors. Let's weave a tapestry of characters that reflects the richness of human experience. Let's give a voice to those who may struggle to be heard. Let's create a literary landscape where everyone feels seen, respected, and understood, because after all, the written word transcends limitations – it celebrates the power of communication, in all its beautiful complexity.

For More Information:

Developmental language

- **American Speech-Language Hearing Association**: https://www.asha.o rg/practice-portal/clinical-topics/spoken-language-disorders/
- **Center for Disease Control Developmental language:** https://www.cdc. gov/ncbddd/developmentaldisabilities/language-disorders.html
- **National Institute on Deafness and Other Communication Disorders - Developmental Language Disorder:** https://www.nidcd.nih.gov/health /developmental-language-disorder
- **National Institute on Deafness and Other Communication Disorders - Speech and Language:** https://www.nidcd.nih.gov/health/speech-and-language
- **National Institute on Deafness and Other Communication Disorders - Autism Spectrum Disorder:** https://www.nidcd.nih.gov/health/autism-spectrum-disorder-communication-problems-children

Aphasia

- **Mayo Clinic:** https://www.mayoclinic.org/diseases-conditions/aphas ia/symptoms-causes/syc-20369518
- **John Hopkins Medicine:** https://www.hopkinsmedicine.org/health/co nditions-and-diseases/aphasia
- **American Speech-Language Hearing Association:** https://www.asha.o rg/public/speech/disorders/aphasia/
- **My stroke of insight**: https://youtu.be/-GsVhbmecJA?si=QlYSqQEzfSB tS2xv
- **Patience, Listening and Communicating with Aphasia Patients:** https://youtu.be/aPTTjRTmgqo?si=ocrdBy9fGiyRVR92
- **Living with Stroke Survivor Stories - Aphasia:** https://youtu.be/LouAl

dbmhHM?si=sPuXUTDJ8cPzckou
- **Broca's Aphasia (Non-Fluent Aphasia):** https://youtu.be/JWC-cVQmE mY?si=pDRc5n0x20n4vlCV

Traumatic Brain Injury (TBI) - includes concussions

- **Center for Disease Control:** https://www.cdc.gov/TraumaticBrainInju ry/
- **Concussions are elusive and invisible injuries**: https://youtu.be/gSlabK LyjDE?si=_6OWH9dCDCXaOIX7
- **American Speech-Language Hearing Association:** https://www.asha.o rg/public/speech/disorders/traumatic-brain-injury/

Character Checklist: Language Disorders

This checklist is designed to help you develop a character with a language disorder in a sensitive and authentic way.

Character Background:

- Specific Language Disorder: What type of language disorder does your character have? (e.g., Aphasia, Specific Language Impairment (SLI), Expressive Language Disorder, Receptive Language Disorder)
- Age of Onset: When did the language disorder develop (childhood, adulthood)? Was there a triggering event (e.g., stroke, brain injury)?
- When were they diagnosed? Who diagnosed them? What was the professional's attitude toward the disorder? How did they feel about the diagnosis? Were they given advice/recommendations?
- Severity: How severe is the language disorder? Does it affect all aspects of language (vocabulary, grammar, comprehension) or is it more specific?
- Cause (if known): Is there a known cause for the language disorder (e.g., developmental delay, neurological condition)?

Language Skills:

- Comprehension: Does your character understand spoken language? If not, to what extent?
- Expressive Language: Can your character express themselves clearly? Do they struggle with vocabulary, grammar, or sentence structure?
- Reading: Can your character read and understand written language? If not, to what extent?
- Writing: Can your character write effectively? Do they struggle with spelling, grammar, or expressing their thoughts clearly?
- Social Language: Does your character understand and use social cues effectively? Do they struggle with turn-taking or maintaining conversations?

Communication Strategies:

- Self-Monitoring: Is your character aware of their language difficulties? Do they try to compensate or avoid certain situations? What strategies do they use when communication fails?
- Alternative Communication: Does your character use alternative communication methods (e.g., assistive devices, gestures, pictures) to supplement speech?
- Speech Therapy: Has your character received speech therapy? If so, how has it impacted their communication skills?

Emotional Impact:

- Frustration: Does your character experience frustration due to their communication limitations?
- Isolation: Does the language disorder lead to social isolation or difficulty making friends?
- Confidence: How does the language disorder impact your character's self-confidence and ability to communicate effectively?

- Misunderstandings: How does your character react when others misunderstand them?
- What does the character wish others knew?

Additional Considerations:

- Impact on Education/Work: Does the language disorder affect your character's education or ability to work?
- Support System: Does your character have a supportive family, friends, or educators who understand their communication needs?
- Character Development: How does the language disorder shape your character's personality, coping mechanisms, and learning strategies?

Narrative Choices:

- Dialogue: How will you represent your character's language disorder in writing (limited vocabulary, grammatical errors, use of alternative communication methods)?
- Internal Monologue: Will you use internal monologue to explore your character's inner thoughts and frustrations with communication?
- Balance: Have you balanced authenticity with the need for clear and engaging storytelling?

Character Development:

- Strengths and Struggles: How does your character's language disorder impact their daily life and interactions with others?
- Beyond Language: What are your character's strengths and personality traits beyond their language disorder?
- Avoid Stereotypes: Have you avoided relying solely on their language disorder to define your character?

Representation:

- Respectful Portrayal: Have you portrayed your character's language disorder with respect and sensitivity?
- Avoidance of Caricatures: Have you avoided stereotypical or exaggerated representations of people with language disorders?
- Choices: Did you give your character choices in treatment and coping strategies?

Remember:

- This checklist is a starting point; not all characters with language disorders will experience all of these aspects.
- Research the specific language disorder to ensure an accurate portrayal.
- Consider including resources for readers who want to learn more,
- Focus on your character's unique strengths, resilience, and alternative communication methods.

Challenge Accepted: Stepping into a World of Limited Language for a Day to Deepen Your Characters

Crafting characters with language disorders requires a keen understanding of their challenges. Research is vital, but to truly connect with their experience, consider this challenge: **spend a day navigating with limited language.**

Understanding Language Disorders

Language disorders affect a person's ability to understand or express language. This can manifest in various ways, from difficulty finding the right words to challenges with grammar or sentence structure.

The Challenge: 24 Hours of Limited Language

For 24 hours, intentionally restrict your language use to simulate the experience of a language disorder. Here are some ways to achieve this:

- Limited Vocabulary: Choose a set of 100-200 common words and restrict your communication to those words only.
- Simple Sentence Structure: Use basic sentence structures like subject-verb-object. Avoid complex sentence constructions or clauses.
- Charades & Gestures: When struggling to find words, rely on gestures and charades to convey your meaning.
- Limited Reading & Writing: Minimize reading and writing, focusing on spoken communication with your chosen limitations.

Why Experience Limited Language?

- Empathy Through Experience: This challenge isn't meant to mimic a specific disorder. It's about understanding the frustration of struggling to express yourself clearly.
- Beyond Stereotypes: Language disorders are diverse. This exercise broadens your perspective on how limited language can impact a character's communication.
- Respectful Representation: By experiencing the limitations, you gain a deeper appreciation for the creativity and alternative communication strategies people with language disorders develop.

Important Considerations:

- Sensitivity: This challenge is about learning, not mockery. Be mindful of the realities of language disorders and avoid perpetuating stereotypes.
- Frustration is Expected: This experience might be frustrating. Remember, the goal is to gain understanding, not mastery.
- Focus on Communication: Despite the limitations, strive to communi-

cate your needs and ideas effectively.

The Power of Vulnerability

This challenge isn't about replicating a medical condition. It's about opening yourself up to a new reality. By experiencing the limitations of language difficulties, even for a day, you'll gain a deeper understanding of the characters you create.

This empathy will translate into richer, more authentic portrayals, ensuring your characters with language disorders are not defined by their struggles, but by their resilience and creative spirit.

Are you ready to accept the challenge?

8

Hearing Impairments

When the World Quiets: Understanding Hearing and Vestibular Disorders

I magine a character struggling to follow a conversation at a party, the music a muffled blur. Or perhaps they experience dizziness that disrupts their sense of balance. These challenges could be due to hearing or vestibular disorders, affecting how we perceive sound and navigate the world.

This section dives into the nature of hearing and vestibular disorders, equipping you, the author, to create authentic characters who navigate these challenges. By understanding the spectrum of hearing loss and the complexities of vestibular disorders, you can craft relatable characters who add depth and richness to your stories.

Please note:

The information presented in this book is intended to provide writers with a general understanding of communication disorders. It is not a replacement for a professional evaluation by a qualified Speech-Language Pathologist (SLP). If you suspect someone may have a communication disorder, please consult with an SLP for diagnosis and treatment recommendations.

When the World Sounds Different: A Guide to Hearing and Vestibular Disorders

Imagine a character struggling to follow a conversation at a party, the music a muffled blur. Or picture them experiencing dizziness that disrupts their sense of balance. These challenges could be due to hearing or vestibular disorders, affecting how we perceive sound and navigate the world.

This section dives into the different types of hearing and vestibular disorders, equipping you, the author, to create authentic characters who face these challenges.

By understanding the spectrum of hearing loss and the complexities of vestibular issues, you can craft relatable characters who add depth and richness to your stories.

The Spectrum of Hearing Loss

Hearing loss isn't a one-size-fits-all condition. Here's a breakdown of some common types:

Conductive Hearing Loss

This occurs when something blocks sound waves from reaching the inner ear. It can be caused by earwax buildup, ear infections, or structural abnormalities. Characters with conductive loss might experience sounds as muffled or quieter, especially in noisy environments. The good news? It's often treatable with medication or surgery.

Sensorineural Hearing Loss

This type of hearing loss involves damage to the inner ear or the auditory nerve pathways. It can be caused by aging, loud noise exposure, genetics, or medical conditions.

Characters with sensorineural loss might struggle to understand speech, especially in noisy situations. They may also have trouble pinpointing where sounds come from or distinguishing between similar sounds. While not curable, hearing aids or cochlear implants can significantly improve their communication and quality of life.

Mixed Hearing Loss

As the name suggests, this is a combination of both conductive and sensorineural factors. Characters with mixed loss might experience a mix of symptoms from both types, making hearing challenging in various situations. Treatment depends on the underlying causes but might involve a combination of medical, surgical, or amplification strategies.

Severity

Hearing loss is typically categorized based on the degree of sound dampening measured in decibels (dB). Here's a breakdown of the different levels:

Normal Hearing (0-20 dB)

This range represents normal hearing ability. People in this range can hear sounds as quiet as a whisper and comfortably understand conversations.

Mild Hearing Loss (21-40 dB)

At this level, some quiet sounds like faint conversation or birds chirping might be difficult to hear. Speech can still be understood in most quiet settings.

Moderate Hearing Loss (41-60 dB)

Conversations become more challenging, especially in noisy environments. Individuals with moderate hearing loss might miss softer sounds like consonants or high-pitched tones. They may rely on lipreading or ask others to repeat themselves frequently.

Severe Hearing Loss (61-80 dB)

Normal conversation is difficult to understand without amplification. Individuals with severe hearing loss might only perceive loud sounds or muffled speech. They often rely heavily on lipreading and hearing aids for communication.

Profound Hearing Loss (81 dB or greater)

At this level, severe hearing loss makes it difficult to detect even loud sounds without amplification. Individuals with profound hearing loss might rely heavily on sign language or other forms of assistive communication technology.

*It's important to note: These are general classifications, and individual experiences with hearing loss can vary. **Different frequencies (pitches) of sound can be affected unevenly.** Someone might have trouble hearing high-pitched sounds but perceive lower tones relatively well, even within the same hearing loss category. Refer to a **speech banana** for information on which speech sounds are affected by the loss of different frequencies, such as the following: https://ohns.ucsf.edu/audiology/education/peds

Beyond Hearing: Understanding Tinnitus

Tinnitus isn't hearing loss, but it can often accompany it. It's the perception of ringing, buzzing, or other noises in the ears, even when no external sound is present.

Imagine your character experiencing a constant hum or a high-pitched whistle – that's tinnitus. While the exact cause is unknown, it's often linked to hearing loss, noise exposure, or other medical conditions. There's no cure, but sound therapy, cognitive-behavioral therapy, and lifestyle changes can help manage the symptoms.

Keeping Your Balance: Vestibular Disorders

The vestibular system is our inner ear's balance center. When this system malfunctions, it can lead to a range of vestibular disorders affecting balance, spatial orientation, and coordination.

- **Benign Paroxysmal Positional Vertigo (BPPV):** This common disorder causes brief episodes of vertigo, a spinning sensation, triggered by specific head movements. Imagine your character getting dizzy after looking up to grab a book on a high shelf – that's BPPV. Luckily, it's often treatable with simple repositioning maneuvers.
- **Meniere's Disease:** This chronic disorder causes recurring episodes of vertigo, fluctuating hearing loss, tinnitus, and a feeling of fullness in the ear. Characters with Meniere's might experience a sudden attack of dizziness accompanied by changes in their hearing and a feeling of pressure in their ear.
- **Vestibular Neuritis and Labyrinthitis:** These inflammatory conditions affect the balance nerves or inner ear structures. They typically come on suddenly, causing severe vertigo, nausea, vomiting, and imbalance.

Characters with these conditions might experience a debilitating spinning sensation along with other unpleasant symptoms.

Hearing the World Differently: Auditory Processing Disorder (APD)

People with APD have normal hearing sensitivity, but their brains struggle to process and understand auditory information effectively. This can lead to difficulties with:

- **Speech in Noise:** Imagine your character straining to follow a conversation at a crowded restaurant. This is a common challenge for people with APD. Background noise makes it difficult to separate speech sounds from other sounds.
- **Auditory Discrimination:** Characters with APD might have trouble distinguishing between similar sounds, like "bat" and "cat." This can make understanding spoken language challenging.
- **Auditory Memory:** Remembering instructions or following a series of spoken directions can be difficult for individuals with APD. They might miss important details or struggle to recall information presented verbally.

By understanding these different hearing and vestibular disorders, you can create characters whose experiences feel real and relatable. Remember, these challenges don't define a person – they're simply part of their unique story.

Why We Hear Differently: Causes of Hearing Loss, Tinnitus, Vestibular Disorders, and APD

Understanding why characters experience hearing loss, tinnitus, vestibular disorders, or APD is crucial for crafting authentic portrayals. Here's a breakdown of the contributing factors:

Hearing Loss: A Matter of Timing

Hearing loss can be categorized into two main groups: congenital and acquired.

Congenital Hearing Loss: Present at birth or develops shortly after.

- **Genetics:** Inherited from parents due to mutations affecting the auditory system.
- **Prenatal Factors:** Maternal infections (rubella, cytomegalovirus) or toxins during pregnancy.
- **Perinatal Factors:** Premature birth, low birth weight, or complications during delivery.

Acquired Hearing Loss: Develops later in life due to various factors.

- **Noise Exposure:** Loud noises (machinery, firearms, concerts) damage the inner ear over time.
- **Aging: Presbycusis** (age-related hearing loss) is common and affects the inner ear and auditory nerve.
- **Medical Conditions:** Ototoxicity (medication damage), Meniere's disease, or autoimmune disorders can contribute.
- **Ear Fluid and Infections:** Feeling like your ears are full or having trouble hearing clearly? Fluid buildup behind the eardrum, called otitis media with effusion, can happen due to colds, allergies, or problems with the Eustachian tube, which drains fluid from the middle ear into the throat.

This can cause mild to moderate hearing loss. Repeated ear infections can lead to eardrum perforation (a hole in the eardrum) or scarring, leading to more severe hearing loss.

Tinnitus: The Ringing Enigma

Tinnitus isn't hearing loss, but it can accompany it. It's the perception of ringing, buzzing, or other noises in the ears, even in silence. Here's what might cause it:

- Loud Noise Exposure
- Age-Related Hearing Loss
- Ear Infections
- Underlying Medical Conditions (cardiovascular or neurological disorders)

Vestibular Disorders: When Your Balance Goes Awry

The vestibular system is your inner ear's balance center. When it malfunctions, you get vestibular disorders affecting balance and spatial orientation. Here are some common culprits:

- **Inner Ear Infections:** Labyrinthitis or vestibular neuritis (viral or bacterial) can cause vertigo, dizziness, and imbalance.
- **Benign Paroxysmal Positional Vertigo (BPPV):** Brief episodes of vertigo triggered by head movements due to displaced crystals in the inner ear.
- **Meniere's Disease:** Chronic episodes of vertigo, fluctuating hearing loss, tinnitus, and ear pressure due to fluid buildup or pressure changes in the inner ear.
- **Head Trauma:** Injuries can damage vestibular structures or disrupt neural pathways for balance.
- **Neurological Conditions:** Multiple sclerosis, vestibular migraine, or acoustic neuroma can affect the vestibular system.

- **Medication Side Effects:** Some medications (antibiotics, antidepressants) can have ototoxic effects, leading to dizziness and vertigo.

Auditory Processing Disorder (APD): Hearing But Not Quite Understanding

People with APD have normal hearing sensitivity, but their brains struggle to process and understand sounds effectively. Here's what might contribute:

- **Genetics:** Genetic mutations can impact the structure or function of auditory pathways.
- **Prenatal and Perinatal Factors:** Maternal infections, toxins, complications during childbirth, or premature birth can affect the developing auditory system.
- **Brain Development:** Abnormalities in the auditory pathways or neurological conditions like autism or ADHD can affect processing.
- **Environmental Factors:** Noise pollution, chronic ear infections, or head trauma may increase the risk.
- **Developmental Factors:** Delays in language development, speech sound discrimination, or auditory memory can contribute to APD.

By understanding these causes, you can create characters whose hearing challenges feel real and relatable. Remember, these factors are just part of their story, not the whole picture.

The Impact of Hearing Challenges: Beyond the Ringing and Dizziness

Hearing loss, tinnitus, vestibular disorders, and auditory processing disorders (APDs) all affect how we perceive and interact with the world. Understanding their impact on your characters goes beyond simply describing muffled sounds or dizzy spells. Here's a breakdown of how these challenges can manifest and influence your character's life:

Hearing Loss: A Spectrum of Silence

Hearing loss isn't a one-size-fits-all condition. It can range from barely noticeable to profoundly isolating.

Here are some common struggles characters with hearing loss might face:

- **Muffled Conversations:** Imagine straining to follow a conversation at a dinner party, laughter sounding distant and words blurring together. This can lead to feelings of frustration and social withdrawal.
- **Constant Requests:** "Can you repeat that?" Characters with hearing loss might find themselves asking this frequently, feeling self-conscious or a burden on others.
- **Turning Up the Volume:** The world might seem quieter for them. They may need to crank up the volume on TVs, phones, or music players, which can bother others around them.
- **Isolation and Loneliness:** Difficulty communicating can create social barriers. Characters with hearing loss might isolate themselves to avoid feeling left out or misunderstood.

Tinnitus: The Unwanted Guest in Your Ears

Tinnitus isn't hearing loss, but it can often accompany it. It's the perception of a constant ringing, buzzing, or hissing in the ears, even in silence. Imagine your character experiencing a never-ending high-pitched whine – that's tinnitus. Here's how it can affect them:

- **Distress and Anxiety:** The relentless nature of tinnitus can be very stressful. It can be difficult to concentrate, sleep, or relax with this constant phantom noise.
- **Irritability and Frustration:** Tinnitus can make it hard to focus on conversations or tasks. This can lead to frustration and irritability, impacting relationships and daily activities.
- **Sleep Disturbances:** Falling asleep and staying asleep can be a challenge with tinnitus. The constant noise can be disruptive, leading to fatigue and impacting overall well-being.

Vestibular Disorders: The World Tilts on its Axis

The vestibular system is our inner ear's balance center. When it malfunctions, it can cause a range of unpleasant sensations. Here's how vestibular disorders can affect your characters:

- **Vertigo and Dizziness:** Imagine feeling like the room is spinning or that you're constantly off-balance. This can be disorienting and scary, making it difficult to walk, drive, or navigate crowded spaces.
- **Anxiety and Fear:** The unpredictable nature of vertigo and dizziness can lead to anxiety and fear of falling. Characters might avoid situations that trigger their symptoms, limiting their independence.
- **Social Withdrawal:** Feeling unsteady and disoriented can make social interaction stressful. Characters might withdraw from activities or events to avoid potential embarrassment or falls.

Auditory Processing Disorder (APD): Hearing But Not Understanding

People with APD have normal hearing sensitivity, but their brains struggle to interpret and process auditory information effectively. Here's what characters with APD might experience:

- **Trouble in Noisy Places:** Following a conversation in a bustling restaurant is a challenge. Background noise makes it difficult to separate speech sounds from other sounds, leading to confusion and frustration.
- **Missing Instructions:** Remembering complex instructions or directions can be tricky. Characters with APD might need things repeated or broken down into smaller steps.
- **Academic Struggles:** Difficulty processing auditory information can impact academic performance. Characters might struggle to follow lectures, take notes, or participate in classroom discussions.
- **Low Self-Esteem:** Feeling misunderstood or unable to keep up can lead to feelings of low self-esteem and social isolation. Characters with APD might avoid situations that require good listening skills.

By understanding these different manifestations and impacts, you can create characters whose hearing challenges feel real and relatable. Remember, these challenges are just one aspect of their personality. They are strong, resilient individuals who navigate the world in their own unique way.

Demystifying the Maze: How Hearing Disorders Are Diagnosed

Creating a character with a hearing disorder requires understanding how these challenges are identified. This section unveils the steps healthcare professionals take to navigate the intricate path of diagnosis.

The Evaluation Journey: Unveiling the Mystery

The evaluation process for auditory disorders is like piecing together a puzzle. Here's what it typically involves:

- **Medical History Check-Up:** Doctors delve into the character's medical background, looking for clues about past illnesses, injuries, or family history that might contribute to hearing issues.
- **Physical Examination:** The ears, nose, and throat get a thorough inspection to identify any physical abnormalities that could affect hearing.
- **Specialized Tests:** Audiologists or ENT specialists step in with specialized tools to assess hearing function. These might include:
- **Pure-Tone Audiometry:** This test measures the faintest sounds a character can hear at different pitches, creating a map of their hearing sensitivity.
- **Speech Audiometry:** Here, the character listens to words or sentences at varying volumes and backgrounds noises, revealing their ability to understand speech.
- **Tympanometry:** This test evaluates the middle ear's function by measuring its pressure and flexibility.
- **Otoacoustic Emissions Testing:** This painless test that is frequently used with newborns assesses the health of the inner ear hair cells that convert soundwaves into electrical signals for the brain.

By combining these elements, healthcare professionals build a comprehensive picture of the character's hearing abilities.

A Team Effort: Working Together for Answers

Diagnosis isn't a solo act. Here's who collaborates to solve the puzzle:

- **Audiologists:** These specialists are the hearing experts, equipped to conduct audiological tests, interpret results, and recommend treatment plans.

- **ENT Specialists (Ear, Nose, and Throat):** They focus on the medical management of ear-related issues, identifying and treating underlying causes of hearing loss.
- **Speech-Language Pathologists:** When auditory processing is suspected, these professionals assess how well the brain interprets sound. They might also provide speech and language therapy to individuals with hearing loss to improve communication skills.

Sifting Through Possibilities: Differential Diagnosis

Sometimes, symptoms can be misleading. Differential diagnosis involves considering other possibilities:

- **Ruling Out Other Culprits:** Ear infections, structural abnormalities in the ear canal, or even neurological conditions can mimic hearing loss symptoms. Doctors need to rule these out to pinpoint the exact cause.
- **Identifying Co-Existing Conditions:** Hearing loss can sometimes accompany other conditions like vestibular disorders (balance issues) or cognitive decline. Recognizing these co-occurring conditions is crucial for a holistic treatment approach.

By working together and considering all possibilities, the healthcare team can arrive at an accurate diagnosis, paving the way for effective management strategies for your character's hearing challenges.

Finding Solutions: Tools and Techniques for Hearing and Vestibular Challenges

Many effective strategies can help characters navigate the world with hearing or vestibular disorders. This section explores various treatments and interventions to consider for your characters.

Hearing Aids: A Helping Hand for Hearing

Hearing aids are tiny electronic devices that amplify sound, making it easier for characters with hearing loss to perceive their surroundings. They come in a variety of styles, from discreet in-the-ear models to comfortable behind-the-ear options.

Advanced features like **directional microphone**s and **noise cancellation** technology can further enhance speech clarity and reduce background noise in crowded spaces.

While hearing aids can greatly improve the lives of people with hearing loss by amplifying sound, they have limitations. **Background noise** can be distracting, making it difficult to understand speech in noisy environments. Additionally, music and certain high-frequency sounds may not be reproduced accurately.

Beyond Hearing Aids: A World of Assistive Technologies

Hearing aids aren't the only solution. Characters may benefit from additional tools to improve communication in challenging environments.

- **Personal Amplifiers**: Portable devices can boost sound in specific situations, like lectures or movie theaters.
- **FM Systems:** These wireless systems transmit sound directly from a source (like a teacher's microphone) to a receiver worn by the character, cutting through background noise.
- **Loop Systems:** Installed in public venues like meeting rooms or

theaters, loop systems transmit sound directly to a character's hearing aid, enhancing clarity.

- **Captioning Services:** Real-time captions displayed on screens or devices can be a valuable aid for characters with hearing loss by providing a text version of spoken dialogue.

Cochlear Implants: A Different Kind of Hearing

For characters with severe hearing loss, cochlear implants offer a remarkable alternative. Unlike traditional hearing aids that amplify existing sounds, cochlear implants work in a fundamentally different way. These surgically implanted devices bypass damaged hair cells in the inner ear, which are often the culprit behind severe hearing loss.

Instead, cochlear implants directly stimulate the auditory nerve with electrical signals. This process allows individuals to perceive sounds and speech in a way that hearing aids simply cannot. The world comes alive with a new richness, filled with the chirping of birds, the murmur of conversations, and the nuances of human speech.

However, it's important to remember that cochlear implants don't restore normal hearing. The experience of sound can vary, and rehabilitation is often necessary to learn how to interpret these new auditory signals

Surgical Interventions: Advanced Solutions

For the most severe cases, surgical interventions like **Auditory Brainstem Implants (ABIs)** or **Bone Anchored Hearing Aids (BAHAs)** may be considered. ABIs stimulate the auditory nerve directly at the brainstem, while BAHAs transmit sound vibrations through the skull bone to the inner ear.

In the case of children with a case history of multiple ear infections, **Pressure Equalization (PE) tubes** may be surgically inserted to relieve pressure and facilitate drainage of the middle ear, improving hearing. They usually fall out or are removed after several months. Surgical restoration of perforations (holes in the ear drum) may be necessary.

Speech Therapy and Auditory Training: Refining Communication Skills

Treatment goes beyond just hearing the sounds.

Auditory rehabilitation and speech therapy can equip characters with valuable strategies to maximize their communication abilities. This might involve exercises to:

- **Improve auditory training:** Learn to differentiate sounds and identify speech in noisy environments.
- **Enhance speech perception:** Develop skills to understand spoken language more clearly.
- **Boost language development:** Build vocabulary and communication skills, especially for children with hearing loss.
- **Sharpen listening skills:** Learn techniques to focus on specific sounds and improve overall listening comprehension.
- **Refine speech production:** Practice clear pronunciation and enunciation to improve communication effectiveness.

Sign Language and Alternative and Augmentative Communication (AAC): Finding a Voice

For some characters with severe communication challenges, traditional speech-based interventions may not be sufficient.

Alternative and Augmentative Communication (AAC) systems provide tools and techniques for them to express themselves effectively. These can include:

- **Picture communication boards:** These boards display images or symbols that characters can point to or arrange to communicate their needs and wants.

- **Speech-generating devices:** These electronic devices allow characters to communicate by selecting pre-recorded messages or typing words that are then spoken aloud by the device.
- **Sign Language:** A complete and complex language using hand gestures and facial expressions, sign language can be a valuable communication tool for characters who are deaf or hard of hearing.

Explore more about Sign Language and AAC in Chapter 11.

By understanding these treatment and intervention options, you can create characters with hearing or vestibular disorders who are resourceful and capable. Remember, these challenges are just one aspect of their lives. With the right support, they can overcome obstacles and thrive in their own unique way.

Debunking the Myths: Understanding Hearing and Vestibular Impairments

Hearing and vestibular impairments can affect a person's ability to hear sounds, maintain balance, and experience spatial orientation. These conditions can be complex, and unfortunately, many myths surround them.

Let's explore 15 common misconceptions to create a clearer understanding:

Hearing Impairment Myths:

- **Myth: Hearing loss means complete deafness.**

Reality: Hearing loss exists on a spectrum, ranging from mild (difficulty hearing faint sounds) to profound (limited or no ability to detect sound). Even individuals with profound hearing loss may have some residual hearing.

- **Myth: Profound hearing loss, or deafness, is always silent.**

Reality: People with profound hearing loss may experience tinnitus, a ringing or buzzing sensation in the ears. This can be a constant or intermittent presence, offering a different kind of auditory experience. Those who experience profound loss later in life might also have auditory memories that influence their perception.

- **Myth: Hearing loss only affects older adults.**

Reality: Hearing loss can occur at any age due to various factors like genetics, exposure to loud noises, or ear infections.

- **Myth: People with hearing loss can't understand speech at all.**

Reality: While understanding speech can be challenging, many people with hearing loss can still communicate effectively with the use of hearing aids, lip reading, and clear communication strategies.

- **Myth: Anyone who can't hear well can simply read lips.**

In reality, lipreading is a complex skill that only captures a portion of spoken language. Many sounds appear identical on the lips, making it difficult to differentiate words, especially in noisy environments or when the speaker's face is obscured or turned away.

- **Myth: Hearing aids will restore perfect hearing.**

Reality: Hearing aids amplify sounds and improve clarity, but they don't "cure" hearing loss. They can significantly enhance a person's ability to hear and participate in conversations.

- **Myth: Children with hearing loss can't learn to speak.**

Reality: With early intervention and proper support, children with hearing loss can develop strong language skills.

- **Myth: People with hearing loss are less intelligent.**

Reality: Hearing loss affects hearing, not intelligence.

Vestibular Impairment Myths:

- **Myth: Dizziness is always a sign of a vestibular impairment.**

Reality: Dizziness can have various causes, including inner ear problems, medications, and dehydration. However, it can be a prominent symptom of vestibular dysfunction.

- **Myth: People with vestibular impairments always experience vertigo (severe spinning sensation).**

Reality: Vertigo is one type of vestibular symptom, but others include imbalance, nausea, and difficulty focusing vision during movement.

- **Myth: Vestibular impairments only affect older adults.**

Reality: Inner ear problems that cause vestibular dysfunction can occur at any age due to injury, infection, or Meniere's disease.

- **Myth: There's no treatment for vestibular impairments.**

Reality: Vestibular rehabilitation therapy can help individuals with vestibular dysfunction improve their balance and reduce dizziness.

Combined Hearing & Vestibular Myths:

- **Myth: Hearing aids can treat vestibular problems.**

Reality: While some hearing aids have features to address tinnitus (ringing in the ears) associated with vestibular issues, they don't directly treat balance problems.

- **Myth: People with hearing and vestibular impairments are isolated and can't participate in social activities.**

Reality: With proper support, communication strategies, and assistive devices, individuals with these impairments can lead fulfilling social lives.

- **Myth: Hearing loss and vestibular impairments are contagious.**

Reality: These conditions are not infectious. They arise from specific underlying conditions.

- **Myth: People with hearing and vestibular impairments are more likely to experience anxiety or depression.**

Reality: There's no direct causal link. However, the challenges associated with these conditions can contribute to anxiety or low self-esteem. Support groups and open communication can help.

- **Myth: Hearing and vestibular impairments mean a person can't have a successful career.**

Reality: Many individuals with these impairments thrive professionally. With accommodations and open communication with employers, they can excel in various fields.

By understanding these myths, we can create a more inclusive and supportive environment for people with hearing and vestibular impairments.

Bringing Your Characters to Life: Portraying Hearing Diversity with Authenticity

Creating characters with hearing impairments goes beyond simply turning down the volume in their world. It's about capturing the richness of their experiences, challenges, and triumphs. This section explores how to bring these characters to life with authenticity and empathy.

Beyond Silence: Understanding Hearing Loss and Auditory Processing Disorders

Imagine struggling to follow a conversation at a party or having difficulty understanding a teacher's lecture.

Characters with hearing loss or auditory processing disorders (APDs) face these challenges daily. To portray them authentically, explore the nuances of these conditions:

- **Communication Difficulties:** Conversations might feel muffled, speech can seem blurry, and following a group discussion can be exhausting, even with aids.
- **Social Barriers:** Difficulty understanding others can lead to social isolation and feelings of frustration.
- **Coping Mechanisms**: Characters might develop strategies like asking for frequent repetition, seeking quiet environments, or relying on lipreading.

By depicting these challenges with sensitivity, you can foster understanding and show the resilience of your characters.

A Vibrant World: Deaf Culture and Community

Deaf culture is a vibrant and complex world with its own values, traditions, and communication methods. Here are some key aspects to consider for your characters:

- **Language:** Sign language is the primary language of Deaf culture. There are many different sign languages used around the world, and American Sign Language (ASL) is a prominent example. Understanding the importance of sign language and incorporating it authentically can add depth to your characters.
- **Visual Communication:** Deaf culture emphasizes visual communication. Facial expressions, body language, and use of space play a crucial role in conveying emotions and information. Pay attention to how your characters use these visual cues.
- **Community:** Deaf culture fosters a strong sense of community and shared identity. Deaf individuals often build close relationships with others who share their experiences. Consider how your characters connect with the Deaf community.
- **Deaf Gain:** This concept challenges the view of deafness as a disability. Deaf gain emphasizes the unique perspectives and strengths that come with being Deaf. Explore how your characters view their deafness and how it shapes their lives.
- **Technology:** Technology plays a significant role in the lives of Deaf people, offering new ways to communicate, access information, and connect with others. Consider how your characters utilize technology to navigate a hearing world.
- **Attitudes and Advocacy:** Deaf culture faces challenges and discrimination. You can explore how your characters navigate these issues and advocate for inclusion and accessibility.

Here are some additional points to keep in mind:

- **Deaf culture is not monolithic.** There's a diversity of experiences and perspectives within the Deaf community.
- **Not all deaf or hard-of-hearing people identify with Deaf culture.** Some may prioritize spoken language or integrate into mainstream culture.
- **Respectful portrayal is key.** Research Deaf culture and consult with Deaf individuals or organizations for an accurate representation.
- By incorporating these aspects of Deaf culture, you can create well-rounded and authentic characters who enrich your story.

Building Empathy: Researching for Depth

To create characters that resonate with readers, delve deeper. Here are some ways to gain invaluable insights:

- **Personal Stories:** Seek out interviews with individuals with hearing impairments or APDs. Read memoirs or explore online communities.
- **Expert Advice:** Consult with audiologists, educators, and disability specialists who work with these populations.
- **Understanding Technology:** Explore the assistive technologies that play a crucial role in many characters' lives – hearing aids, cochlear implants, and communication devices.

By going beyond the surface level, you'll create characters with depth and nuance.

Empowering Characters: Strength and Resilience

Hearing impairments may present challenges, but they don't define who a character is. Here's how to showcase their strength:

- **Advocacy:** Characters can advocate for themselves and others, challenging societal biases and promoting disability rights.

- **Self-Advocacy Skills:** Characters can navigate social situations and communication barriers effectively, demonstrating their resilience.
- **Community Contributions:** Highlight how characters contribute to their communities, fostering a sense of belonging and empowerment.

By showcasing their advocacy efforts and agency, you'll create characters who inspire readers.

Inclusion Through Understanding

Creating inclusive narratives is key. Here's how to promote understanding:

- **Challenge Stigma:** Depict characters actively challenging misconceptions about hearing impairments.
- **Accessible Environments:** Show the importance of accessible spaces equipped with assistive listening devices or captioning services.
- **Communication Strategies:** Highlight practical communication strategies that can help others interact effectively with characters who have hearing impairments.

By promoting understanding and inclusion, your characters become catalysts for positive change in the world of your story, and perhaps even in the world beyond the page.

Remember, authentic representation is about respect, empathy, and celebrating the rich tapestry of human experience. With these tools, you can craft characters who are not just heard, but understood and celebrated for their unique stories.

The Final Note: Weaving Hearing Diversity into Your Narrative

Our exploration of hearing and communication has painted a vivid picture. We've delved into the complexities of hearing loss, auditory processing disorders (APDs), and the vibrant Deaf culture.

But the journey doesn't end here. This chapter serves as a springboard, empowering you to craft authentic and inclusive portrayals in your writing.

A Spectrum of Experiences: Beyond Silence

Hearing loss isn't a one-size-fits-all condition. It's a spectrum, with each type presenting unique challenges.

The impact of these conditions goes far beyond simply not hearing well. Everyday activities can become a challenge, from following instructions to enjoying a movie. Communication becomes a constant hurdle, leading to feelings of isolation, social anxiety, and even limiting educational and professional opportunities.

Understanding Deaf culture is crucial for creating authentic characters who are deaf or hard of hearing. It's about acknowledging their unique experiences and celebrating the richness within the Deaf community.

Moving Beyond Diagnosis: A Call for Authentic Representation

We've explored the causes, manifestations, and impacts of hearing loss and APDs. Now, let's turn our attention to how they're portrayed in literature.

Unfortunately, characters with hearing impairments are often relegated to one-dimensional roles – the isolated loner, the misunderstood genius, or the object of pity.

This chapter is a call to action. Avoid tired stereotypes like the "deaf villain" or the "magically cured" character. Strive to depict the diverse experiences of individuals with hearing loss and APDs, showcasing their strengths, resilience, and unique perspectives.

Characters with Depth: Building Empathy Through Research

Creating authentic characters requires research and understanding. Here are some ways to gain valuable insights:

- **Personal Stories:** Seek out interviews with individuals with hearing impairments or APDs. Read memoirs or explore online communities.
- **Expert Advice:** Consult with audiologists, educators, and disability specialists who work with these populations.
- **Technology Awareness:** Explore the assistive technologies that play a crucial role in many characters' lives – hearing aids, cochlear implants, and communication devices.

By highlighting the challenges characters face, you can create depth and vulnerability. Depict their struggles in navigating social situations, overcoming communication barriers, or advocating for their needs. This allows readers to connect with them on a deeper level.

Celebrating Diversity: The Power of Inclusive Narratives

The goal is to create inclusive narratives that celebrate diversity and break down barriers. This doesn't mean every character needs to be hearing-impaired, but it does require mindful representation. Inclusive narratives can be achieved in many ways:

- Characters who use sign language

- Characters with mild or partial hearing loss
- Depictions of assistive technologies
- Normalizing the experience of deafness or hearing loss

By creating complex, relatable, and deserving characters with hearing impairments, you can challenge misconceptions and promote understanding.

By embracing diversity, fostering empathy, and actively promoting inclusion, authors can contribute to a world where all voices are heard and valued. Imagine a world where literature reflects the richness of human experience, celebrating every story, every voice, without exception.

That's the power of inclusive storytelling, and you, as the author, hold the key to unlocking it.

For more information:

- **American Speech-Language and Hearing Association:** https://www.asha.org/public/hearing/
- **AG Bell Association:** https://www.agbell.org/Families/Hearing-Loss-Explained
- **Hearing Like Me.com:** https://www.hearinglikeme.com/what-is-an-audiogram/
- **Centers for Disease Control and Prevention:** https://www.cdc.gov/ncbddd/hearingloss/index.html
- **National Institute on Deafness and Other Communication Disorders:** https://www.nidcd.nih.gov/health/hearing-ear-infections-deafness
- **NIDCD Statistics:** https://www.nidcd.nih.gov/health/statistics/quick-statistics-hearing
- **Epidemiology:** https://www.nidcd.nih.gov/health/statistics/what-numbers-mean-epidemiological-perspective-hearing
- **John Hopkins Medicine:** https://www.hopkinsmedicine.org/health/conditions-and-diseases/hearing-loss

- **John Hopkins Medicine Cochlear Implants:** https://www.hopkinsme
dicine.org/health/treatment-tests-and-therapies/cochlear-implants/
childrens-cochlear-implants
- **What You Don't Know About Hearing Aids:** https://youtu.be/0vf1q_
HgLpw?si=ho6MJwoR3wxJnXlF
- **This Is How a Deaf Person's Voice Sounds:** https://youtu.be/3V95p7Et
GCI?si=1WkNzFchbtTQtaJC
- **Deaf People Answer Commonly Googled Questions About Being Deaf:**
https://youtu.be/IgmB9c29UKU?si=WPX5Je76fSIAxSLz
- **What a Cochlear Implant Actually Sounds Like:** https://youtu.be/lzgQr
HFDNLE?si=e-_lxgouUYM6rbPc
- **Hearing & Balance: Crash Course:** https://youtu.be/Ie2j7GpC4JU?si=-
FsIlvAPvHftxw5e
- **Hearing Cochlear Implants**: https://youtu.be/00WOao4kpwM?si=R0Ol
uiO6duuaUS-d
- **local deaf community or school**

Character Checklist: Auditory and Vestibular Disorders

This checklist is designed to help you develop a character with hearing or balance challenges in a sensitive and authentic way.

Character Background:

- Specific Disorder (if known): Does your character have hearing loss (conductive, sensorineural, mixed), Meniere's disease, benign paroxysmal
positional vertigo (BPPV), or another auditory/vestibular disorder?
- Age of Onset: When did the disorder develop (childhood, adulthood)?
Was there a triggering event (e.g., illness, injury, noise exposure)? Did it
prevent them from critical language learning when they were younger?
- When were they diagnosed? Who diagnosed them? What was the
professional's attitude toward the disorder? How did they feel about the
diagnosis? Were they given advice/recommendations?

- Severity: How severe is the disorder? Is your character deaf, hard of hearing, or does their balance have varying degrees of impairment?
- Cause (if known): Is there a known cause for the disorder (e.g., genetics, aging, medication)?

Hearing:

- Degree of Hearing Loss: Can your character hear some sounds or speech clearly? Do they rely on amplification (hearing aids, cochlear implants)?
- Tinnitus: Does your character experience tinnitus (ringing or buzzing in the ears)? If so, how does it affect them?
- Balance:
- Frequency of Dizziness: How often does your character experience dizziness or vertigo? Is it triggered by specific movements?
- Impact on Daily Activities: Does your character's balance problem affect their ability to walk, climb stairs, or drive?

Communication Strategies:

- Self-Monitoring: Is your character aware of their hearing or balance limitations? Do they ask others to speak clearly or avoid certain situations?
- Alternative Communication: Does your character use assistive listening devices (captions, amplified phones) or communication strategies (lipreading, sign language)?
- Visual Cues: Does your character rely on facial expressions and body language to understand communication?
- What do they do when communication fails?

Emotional Impact:

- Frustration: Does your character experience frustration due to communication difficulties or balance problems?
- Isolation: Do hearing or balance challenges lead to social isolation or difficulty participating in activities?
- Confidence: How does the disorder impact your character's self-confidence and sense of independence?
- Anxiety: Does your character experience anxiety in situations where they might struggle to hear or maintain balance?
- What do they wish others knew?

Additional Considerations:

- Support System: Does your character have a supportive family, friends, or colleagues who understand their needs?
- Treatment: Has your character received treatment (hearing aids, physical therapy) for their disorder? If so, how has it impacted them?
- Character Development: How does the auditory/vestibular disorder shape your character's personality, coping mechanisms, and social interactions?

Narrative Choices:

- Sensory Details: How will you describe the world through your character's perspective (limited sounds, visual cues for balance)?
- Internal Monologue: Will you use internal monologue to explore your character's thoughts and anxieties about communication or balance challenges?
- Balance: Have you balanced authenticity with the need for clear and engaging storytelling?

Character Development:

- Strengths and Struggles: How does your character's auditory/vestibular disorder impact their daily life and interactions with others?
- Beyond the Disorder: What are your character's strengths and personality traits beyond their hearing or balance challenges?
- Avoid Stereotypes: Have you avoided relying solely on the disorder to define your character?
- Choices: Have you given your character choices in treatment and coping strategies?

Representation:

- Respectful Portrayal: Have you portrayed your character's disorder with respect and sensitivity?
- Avoidance of Caricatures: Have you avoided stereotypical or exaggerated representations of people with hearing loss or balance disorders?

Remember:

- This checklist is a starting point; not all characters with auditory/vestibular disorders will experience all of these aspects.
- Research the specific disorder to ensure an accurate portrayal.
- Consider including resources for readers who want to learn more.
- Focus on your character's unique strengths, resilience, and coping mechanisms.

Challenge Accepted: Navigating a Day with Simulated Hearing Impairment to Deepen Your Characters

Crafting characters with hearing impairments requires a deep understanding of their unique experiences. Research is crucial, but to truly connect with their challenges, consider this bold proposition: **try simulating hearing impairment for a day.**

Understanding Hearing Impairment

Hearing impairment can range from mild to profound, affecting a person's ability to detect or understand sounds. This can lead to difficulties in communication, social interaction, and situational awareness.

The Challenge: 24 Hours of Limited Hearing

For 24 hours, intentionally limit your auditory experience to simulate various aspects of hearing impairment.

Here are some ways to achieve this:

- **Muffled Sounds:** Wear earplugs with varying levels of noise reduction to experience muffled or distorted sounds.
- **Background Noise:** Play white noise or background music at moderate levels throughout the day to simulate the challenge of focusing on specific sounds in a noisy environment.
- **Limited Conversations:** Restrict conversations to one-on-one settings with quiet environments. Avoid group conversations or crowded spaces where background noise makes listening difficult.
- **Visual Cues:** Pay close attention to facial expressions, body language, and lip movements when communicating, mimicking the reliance on visual cues people with hearing loss may utilize. Or watch a movie with the sound turned very low or even off.

Why Simulate Hearing Impairment?

- **Empathy Through Experience:** This challenge isn't about mimicking a specific medical condition. It's about understanding the frustration of missing sounds or conversations, and the importance of clear communication.
- **Beyond Silence:** Hearing loss manifests in various ways. This exercise broadens your perspective on how it can impact a character's daily life and communication strategies.
- **Respectful Representation:** By experiencing the challenges of limited hearing, you gain a deeper respect for the resilience and communication strategies people with hearing impairments develop.

Important Considerations:

- **Safety:** Be aware of your surroundings at all times, especially in traffic or while crossing streets. Consider keeping one earbud out if necessary.
- **Frustration is Expected:** This experience might be frustrating, especially in group settings. Remember, the goal is to gain understanding, not mastery.
- **Focus on Communication:** Despite the limitations, strive to communicate clearly. Utilize visual cues, ask for clarification, and be patient with yourself and others.

The Power of Vulnerability

This challenge isn't about replicating a medical condition perfectly. It's about opening yourself up to a new reality. By experiencing the limitations of hearing impairment, even for a day, you'll gain a deeper understanding of the characters you create.

This empathy will translate into richer, more authentic portrayals, ensuring your characters with hearing impairments are not defined by their limitations, but by their strength and determination to connect with the world around them.

Are you ready to accept the challenge?

9

Feeding and Swallowing Disorders

When Meals Become a Challenge: Understanding Feeding and Swallowing Disorders

Creating a character who struggles to eat might seem like a simple detail, but for many people, these challenges are a daily reality. This section delves into the complexities of feeding and swallowing disorders, equipping you to portray these experiences with authenticity and empathy.

Feeding Disorders: More Than Picky Eaters

Feeding disorders go beyond a dislike of vegetables. They encompass a range of difficulties that affect an individual's ability to safely and efficiently consume and process food. These challenges can arise at any stage of life, from infancy to adulthood. Here's what feeding disorders might involve:

- **Swallowing Difficulties:** The physical act of moving food from the mouth to the stomach can be problematic.
- **Oral-Motor Issues:** Problems with coordinating the muscles in the mouth and face can interfere with chewing and sucking.

- **Sensory Processing Challenges:** Unusual sensitivities to textures, tastes, or smells can make eating a daunting experience.
- **Behavioral Feeding Patterns:** Difficulties with self-regulation, anxiety, or past negative experiences can lead to resistance or avoidance of mealtimes.

Swallowing Disorders (Dysphagia): A Matter of Safe Passage

Swallowing disorders, also known as dysphagia, focus specifically on the physical process of moving food or liquid from the mouth to the stomach. This seemingly simple act involves a complex orchestration of muscles and nerves.

Dysphagia can disrupt any stage of this journey, including:

- **Oral Preparation:** Chewing food properly before swallowing.
- **Oral Transit:** Moving food from the front to the back of the mouth.
- **Pharyngeal Swallow:** The coordinated movement of the throat muscles to safely propel food down the esophagus.
- **Esophageal Transit:** The smooth muscle contractions that move food through the esophagus to the stomach.

Please note:

The information presented in this book is intended to provide writers with a general understanding of communication disorders. It is not a replacement for a professional evaluation by a qualified Speech-Language Pathologist (SLP). If you suspect someone may have a communication disorder, please consult with an SLP for diagnosis and treatment recommendations.

The Ripple Effect: Impact of Feeding and Swallowing Disorders

The consequences of feeding and swallowing disorders extend far beyond mealtimes. Here's how these challenges can impact an individual's life:

- **Nutritional Deficiencies:** Difficulty swallowing can lead to inadequate intake of essential nutrients, resulting in malnutrition, dehydration, and weight loss.
- **Social Isolation:** The fear of choking or messy mealtimes can lead to social withdrawal and a diminished enjoyment of shared meals.
- **Reduced Quality of Life:** The constant struggle to eat safely and effectively can take a toll on a person's overall well-being and emotional state.

By understanding the complexities of feeding and swallowing disorders, you can craft characters whose struggles resonate with readers. The following sections will explore the causes, treatments, and impact of these conditions on individuals and their families.

A Multitude of Challenges: Exploring Common Feeding and Swallowing Disorders

Understanding the different types of feeding and swallowing disorders is crucial for creating characters whose struggles feel real. This section breaks down some of the most common conditions, categorized by age group and cause.

Pediatric Feeding Disorders: Challenges from the Start

- **Failure to Thrive (FTT):** This isn't simply pickiness – it's a concerning lack of weight gain or growth, often caused by insufficient calorie intake or underlying medical conditions.
- **Infantile Anorexia:** Unlike its adult counterpart, this refers to feeding

difficulties in infants, who may refuse to eat, have limited intake, or show aversion to feeding, impacting their growth and nutrition.

- **Gastroesophageal Reflux (GER) and Gastroesophageal Reflux Disease (GERD):** Spit-up happens, but GERD is chronic reflux that can make feeding uncomfortable for infants, leading to irritability, poor weight gain, and difficulty swallowing.
- **Pediatric Dysphagia:** Swallowing isn't always automatic for young children. This can be due to developmental delays, neurological conditions, or structural issues in the mouth and throat.
- **Fine motor skills** are essential for successful self-feeding in young children. Difficulties with grasping utensils, coordinating hand-to-mouth movements, or manipulating textures in the mouth can lead to frustration and hinder a child's ability to eat independently. These challenges can cause mealtimes to become messy and stressful for both the child and caregiver.

Picky Eaters vs. Selective Eating Disorders: When Preference Becomes a Problem

- **Picky Eating:** Every parent knows this struggle! It's when children have strong preferences or dislikes, often based on sensory factors like texture or taste. While frustrating, it usually doesn't pose a major health risk.
- **Avoidant/Restrictive Food Intake Disorder (ARFID):** This is more serious. Children with ARFID have intense restrictions around food, often due to sensory sensitivities, fear of choking, or lack of interest in eating. This can significantly impact their growth and nutrition.
- **Autism Spectrum Disorder (ASD):** Individuals with ASD may have sensory sensitivities that make certain foods or textures unpleasant. They may also struggle with social aspects of mealtimes or routines.

Adult Feeding Disorders: A Spectrum of Challenges

Swallowing Difficulties (Dysphagia)

Swallowing can become problematic in adulthood due to various reasons.

- **Oropharyngeal Dysphagia:** This affects the mouth and throat stages of swallowing, often caused by neurological conditions, structural issues, or muscle weakness.
- **Esophageal Dysphagia:** Problems within the esophagus itself, like narrowing or obstruction, can make swallowing difficult, causing food to stick or chest pain.

Neurological Conditions and Swallowing:

- **Stroke:** Damage from a stroke can affect the brain regions controlling swallowing, leading to difficulty and an increased risk of aspiration pneumonia (fluid in the lungs).
- **Parkinson's Disease:** This neurodegenerative disorder can impair swallowing coordination and cause drooling, impacting nutrition and potentially leading to respiratory complications.
- **Multiple Sclerosis (MS):** MS can affect the brainstem and nerves involved in swallowing, resulting in dysphagia and an increased risk of aspiration.

Gastrointestinal Disorders and Feeding:

- **GERD:** Chronic acid reflux can irritate the esophagus, making swallowing uncomfortable and causing symptoms like heartburn and regurgitation. It can lead to pre-cancerous conditions such as Barrett's Syndrome.
- **Gastroparesis:** Delayed stomach emptying can lead to nausea, vomiting, and difficulty with solid foods, impacting nutrition and quality of life.
- **Inflammatory Bowel Disease (IBD):** Crohn's disease and ulcerative colitis can cause inflammation and structural changes in the digestive tract, leading to pain, diarrhea, and difficulty absorbing nutrients, all of

which can affect feeding and overall health.

- **Rumination Syndrome:** This less common disorder involves the repeated regurgitation of previously swallowed food, often associated with emotional distress.
- **Fine motor limitations** can also disrupt feeding in adults. Individuals with tremors, weakness, or decreased dexterity may struggle to hold utensils, open packaging, or manage certain food textures. This can lead to dependence on others for assistance with feeding and a diminished sense of independence at mealtimes.

Remember, this is not an exhaustive list, but it provides a foundation for understanding the diverse challenges characters with feeding and swallowing disorders can face. The following sections will delve deeper into the causes, treatments, and impact of these conditions on individuals and their families.

When the Body Betrays: Causes of Feeding and Swallowing Disorders

Understanding why a character might struggle to eat goes beyond physical limitations. This section explores the neurological, structural, and environmental factors that can contribute to feeding and swallowing disorders.

The Brain-Body Connection: Neurological Factors

Our nervous system orchestrates the complex dance of swallowing. When this intricate network is disrupted by neurological conditions, difficulties can arise. Here are some common culprits:

- **Stroke:** Damage caused by a stroke can affect the brain regions controlling swallowing, leading to dysphagia and an increased risk of aspiration.
- **Traumatic Brain Injury (TBI):** A head injury can disrupt the nerves and pathways crucial for swallowing coordination.
- **Neurodegenerative Diseases:** Conditions like Parkinson's and

Alzheimer's can impair muscle control and coordination, impacting chewing and swallowing.

- **Neuromuscular Disorders:** Muscular dystrophy and ALS weaken the muscles involved in swallowing, making it difficult to move food safely through the digestive tract.

Structural Obstacles: When Anatomy Creates Challenges

Sometimes, the physical structure of the mouth, throat, or esophagus can present challenges. Here's what to consider:

- **Tumors:** Growths in the head and neck region can obstruct the passage of food or disrupt the delicate swallowing mechanism.
- **Anatomical Abnormalities:** Birth defects like cleft lip and palate or structural malformations can interfere with proper swallowing function.
- **Surgical Interventions and Radiation Therapy:** Surgeries or radiation treatment for head and neck cancers can leave scar tissue or alter the anatomy, impacting swallowing.

Trauma: A Sudden Disruption

Injuries to the head, neck, or chest can damage the nerves, muscles, or bones involved in swallowing. These can be caused by:

- Motor vehicle accidents
- Falls
- Sports injuries

The severity and location of the trauma will determine the extent of feeding and swallowing difficulties. These challenges may be temporary or long-term.

By understanding these causes, you can create characters whose struggles feel genuine and illustrate the impact of feeding and swallowing disorders on their lives.

The following sections will explore treatment options, coping strategies, and the emotional toll these conditions can take on individuals and their families.

Beyond the Physical: The Ripple Effects of Feeding and Swallowing Disorders

Feeding and swallowing disorders aren't just messy or inconvenient – they can have a profound impact on a person's life. This section explores the physical signs, functional limitations, and emotional consequences these conditions can bring.

Warning Signs: Recognizing Swallowing Difficulties

The body often sends out warning signals when swallowing isn't working properly. Here are some key symptoms to watch for:

- **Difficulty initiating a swallow:** Food might seem to sit in the mouth for a long time before being swallowed.
- **Problems forming a food bolus:** The chewed food mass may be difficult to form or manipulate in the mouth.
- **Signs of aspiration:** Coughing or choking during swallowing could indicate food or liquids entering the airway instead of the stomach.
- **Malnutrition:** Difficulty consuming enough food and drinks can lead to deficiencies in essential nutrients and calories.

More Than Just Eating: The Functional Impact

Feeding and swallowing disorders go beyond the act of eating. They can significantly impact daily life in these ways:

- **Challenges with maintaining hydration:** Swallowing difficulties can make it hard to drink enough fluids, leading to dehydration.
- **Difficulties with medications:** Swallowing pills or liquid medications can become a hurdle for some individuals.

The Emotional Toll: Social Isolation and Beyond

The frustration, anxiety, and even fear associated with feeding and swallowing disorders can have a significant emotional impact that extends far beyond the dinner table. Here's a closer look at how these disorders can affect a person's well-being:

Social Isolation:

- **Fear of Choking:** The constant threat of choking can lead people to avoid social situations that involve eating, like restaurants, potlucks, or even family dinners. This withdrawal can create feelings of isolation and loneliness.
- **Embarrassment and Anxiety:** Individuals with feeding disorders may be embarrassed by the amount of time it takes to eat, the need for specialized utensils, or the fear of messy accidents. This anxiety can make them avoid social gatherings altogether.
- **Cultural Pressures:** In many cultures, food is central to social interaction and celebration. Missing out on shared meals due to a feeding disorder can be especially isolating and can lead to feelings of exclusion. For example, some cultures emphasize large family meals or festive gatherings around food, making it particularly challenging for those with feeding difficulties.

Psychological Distress:

- **Loss of Control:** Feeding disorders can rob individuals of a sense of control over their own bodies. The inability to eat safely or comfortably can be incredibly frustrating and lead to feelings of helplessness.
- **Low Self-Esteem:** The constant struggle with eating can damage a person's self-esteem, especially for children who may be teased or ostracized by peers.
- **Depression and Anxiety:** The emotional toll of managing a feeding disorder can contribute to the development of depression and anxiety. The constant worry and stress can negatively impact a person's overall mental health.

Cultural Considerations:

- **Body Image:** Cultural standards around body image can be exacerbated by feeding disorders. In cultures that emphasize thinness, individuals with feeding disorders who struggle to maintain a certain weight may experience additional anxiety and shame.
- **Family Dynamics:** Family meals hold significant meaning in many cultures. Feeding disorders can disrupt these traditions and create tension within family dynamics, especially if there's a lack of understanding about the disorder.
- **Stigma and Misconceptions:** In some cultures, there may be a stigma associated with mental health issues, which can lead individuals to avoid seeking help for the emotional impact of their feeding disorder.

By understanding these multifaceted emotional and cultural aspects, you can develop characters with feeding disorders whose struggles feel real and relatable. The following sections will explore treatment options, coping strategies, and the importance of emotional support for individuals and their families.

Cracking the Code: Unveiling Feeding and Swallowing Disorders

Diagnosing a feeding or swallowing disorder involves a detective-like approach. A team of specialists works together to gather clues, using various tools and techniques, to pinpoint the exact cause of the challenges.

This section will equip you to portray these assessments with accuracy and avoid overly technical jargon.

Diagnosing Feeding and Swallowing Issues: A Team Approach

Ensuring safe and efficient swallowing is crucial for good health and well-being. When concerns arise about feeding or swallowing difficulties, a team of healthcare professionals often collaborates to diagnose the underlying issue and develop an appropriate treatment plan.

The Core Team:

- **Speech-Language Pathologists (SLPs):** These specialists take the lead role in swallowing and feeding assessments. They evaluate muscle strength and coordination in the mouth and throat, assess oral motor skills, and determine if there are any neurological or developmental reasons impacting safe swallowing.
- **Occupational Therapists (OTs):** OTs play a vital role, particularly when there are concerns about feeding mechanics, positioning, or the use of adaptive equipment. They can assess a patient's ability to safely navigate the act of eating, including coordination, use of utensils, and maintaining proper posture during meals. They can also recommend and train individuals on the use of adaptive equipment to optimize feeding independence.

Additional Specialists:

- **Pediatricians:** For children with feeding and swallowing difficulties, pediatricians can provide a comprehensive medical evaluation and rule out any underlying medical conditions that might contribute to the issues.
- **Gastroenterologists:** If there are concerns about digestive problems impacting swallowing, a gastroenterologist might be involved to assess the gastrointestinal system.
- **Neurologists:** In cases where there's a suspicion of neurological impairments affecting swallowing, a neurologist may be consulted to perform evaluations and explore potential neurological causes.
- **Dietitians:** Registered dietitians can play a crucial role in developing a safe and appropriate feeding plan, considering any dietary restrictions or nutritional needs related to the swallowing difficulties.

By working together, this team of specialists can provide a comprehensive evaluation, pinpoint the root cause of the feeding or swallowing issue, and develop a collaborative treatment plan to address the patient's specific needs.

The Swallowing Sleuth's Toolkit

SLPs have a variety of tools at their disposal to assess swallowing function.

Clinical Swallowing Evaluation (CSE): A thorough examination of the muscles, reflexes, and nerves involved in swallowing.

- **Case History:** This is where you learn about the person's experience – their feeding habits, any difficulties they've noticed, and their medical background.
- **Oral Motor Exam:** The SLP checks the strength and coordination of the lips, tongue, and cheeks, essential for maneuvering food in the mouth.
- **Swallowing Screening:** This might involve observing the person

swallow different textures of food or liquids, looking for signs of aspiration (food or drink going into the airway).

· **Water Swallow Test:** This simple test assesses how well the person tolerates different volumes of water.

However, none of these guarantee safe swallowing. More advanced instrumental evaluations are preferred for a definitive diagnosis.

High-Tech Help: Instrumental Assessments

· **Videofluoroscopic Swallowing Studies (VFSS)/Modified Barium Swallow (MBS):** Imagine an X-ray movie! The person swallows a contrast material while X-rays capture the movement of food through the throat and esophagus. This reveals how well the muscles are coordinating and if any aspiration occurs.

· **Fiberoptic Endoscopic Evaluation of Swallowing (FEES):** A thin, flexible tube with a camera is passed through the nose to directly view the throat and larynx during swallowing. This allows for a close-up look at the structures involved and helps identify specific abnormalities.

Unveiling the Culprit: Differential Diagnosis

Not every cough during a meal signifies a swallowing disorder. SLPs are trained detectives, differentiating between a primary swallowing disorder and symptoms caused by other conditions such as neurological disorders or respiratory problems.

A Multifaceted Approach: Identifying Co-existing Conditions

Sometimes, feeding difficulties arise from a combination of factors. The team might identify co-existing conditions like GERD (acid reflux) or esophageal motility disorders that can make swallowing more challenging. Addressing these conditions is crucial for a successful treatment plan.

By understanding the evaluation process, you can craft scenes that depict the collaborative effort required to diagnose feeding and swallowing disorders. The following sections will explore treatment options, coping strategies, and the emotional impact on those affected.

Reclaiming the Ability to Swallow: Treatment Options for Feeding and Swallowing Disorders

When a character struggles to eat, it can be more than just physical – it can be a source of frustration and limitation. This section explores the tools speech-language pathologists (SLPs) and other specialists use to help people regain control and improve their quality of life.

The Therapy Toolbox: Techniques for Dysphagia

SLPs are the champions for those with swallowing difficulties (dysphagia). Their treatment plans are tailored to the cause and severity of the problem, with the overall goal of:

- Swallowing safely and efficiently
- Reducing the risk of aspiration (food or liquid entering the lungs)
- Boosting nutritional intake
- Strengthening oral motor function
- Improving overall quality of life

Here's a glimpse into the SLP's toolkit:

Rehabilitative Techniques: These exercises aim to strengthen and retrain the muscles involved in swallowing. This might include:

- **Swallowing Exercises:** Just like any muscle, those used in swallowing can be strengthened with practice. These exercises target coordination, endurance, and overall function.

217

- **Oral Motor Therapy:** The muscles of the mouth and face also play a role. This therapy helps improve their strength and coordination to better manage food in the mouth.

Compensatory Techniques: Sometimes, a different approach is necessary. These techniques help people swallow more safely and efficiently, even with limitations:

- **Modified Diets:** This is a cornerstone. By adjusting the thickness of liquids and texture of solids, swallowing becomes easier and safer.
- **Thickened Liquids:** Special thickeners create consistencies like nectar-thick or pudding-thick, suitable for varying degrees of dysphagia.
- **Solid Food Texture Modifications:** Chopping, grinding, puréing, or moistening foods creates a manageable texture for swallowing.

Postural Techniques: Specific head and body positions can optimize the swallow.

- **Chin Tuck:** Tilting the chin down tightens throat muscles, improving airway closure during swallowing.
- **Head Rotation:** A slight turn to one side may improve food direction for a more efficient swallow.

Swallowing Maneuvers: These are specific actions taken just before or during a swallow to enhance its effectiveness.

- **Supraglottic Swallow:** A brief breath hold during swallowing helps close the airway and prevent aspiration.
- **Effortful Swallow:** A stronger, more forceful swallow may be used to propel food more effectively.

Other Techniques:

- **Pacing:** Taking smaller bites and allowing more time between swallows improves control and safety.
- **Sensory Cues:** Visual or tactile cues (seeing food or feeling the spoon on the lips) can trigger the swallow reflex.

Beyond Therapy: A Multifaceted Approach to Swallowing Disorders

While therapy plays a crucial role in managing swallowing difficulties, a comprehensive approach often involves various interventions tailored to the specific needs of the individual. Here's a look at some options beyond therapy:

Medical Management

Medications: Certain medications can be helpful in addressing underlying conditions that contribute to dysphagia. These might include medications to:

- Improve muscle strength or coordination (e.g., medications for neuro-muscular disorders)
- Reduce excessive secretions in the mouth and throat (e.g., anticholinergics)
- Manage neurological conditions impacting swallowing (e.g., medications for Parkinson's disease)

Nutritional Support:Tube Feeding: In cases where safe oral intake is not possible or insufficient to meet nutritional needs, enteral tube feeding can be a lifesaving intervention. This involves providing nutrition through a feeding tube placed in the stomach or small intestine. There are different types of tube feeding, and the choice depends on factors like:

- The duration of feeding support needed (short-term vs. long-term)

- The patient's medical condition and ability to tolerate different feeding methods (e.g., nasogastric tube, gastrostomy tube)

Surgical Interventions:Endoscopic Procedures: Minimally invasive endoscopic procedures might be used to address certain structural problems in the throat or esophagus that contribute to swallowing difficulties. For example:

- Dilation procedures can be performed to widen a narrowed esophagus (e.g., esophageal dilation)
- Stenting procedures can be used to keep the esophagus open (e.g., esophageal stenting)

Surgical Reconstruction: In some cases, more complex surgical reconstruction might be necessary to correct anatomical abnormalities that affect swallowing. This could involve procedures to:

- Repair structural defects in the throat or esophagus (e.g., pharyngeal flap surgery)
- Improve the function of the swallowing muscles (e.g., myotomy procedures)
- By combining therapy with appropriate medical management, nutritional support, and potential surgical interventions when necessary, healthcare professionals can create a comprehensive treatment plan to optimize swallowing function and quality of life for individuals with dysphagia.

Addressing the Root Cause: Treatment for Specific Conditions

While the techniques above provide a general framework, treatment plans are often tailored to the specific condition:

Pediatric Feeding Disorders (PFD)

For children with PFD, therapists might use:

- **Exposure Therapy:** Gradually introducing new foods and textures in a safe and controlled way.
- **Positive Reinforcement:** Rewarding desired eating behaviors to encourage progress.
- **Mealtime Routines:** Establishing predictable and calming mealtimes to reduce anxiety.
- **Play-based Therapy:** Using play activities to explore food in a non-threatening way.
- **Sensory Integration Therapy:** Helping children with sensory sensitivities become more comfortable with different textures and smells of food.

Avoidant/Restrictive Food Intake Disorder (ARFID)

For children with ARFID, the focus might be on:

- **Cognitive Behavioral Therapy (CBT):** Identifying and modifying negative thoughts and beliefs about food.
- **Exposure Therapy:** Similar to PFD, gradually introducing new foods in a safe and supportive environment.
- **Family Therapy:** Helping families develop positive mealtime interactions to reduce stress and anxiety.

Eating Disorders (Anorexia Nervosa and Bulimia Nervosa)

Treatment for eating disorders typically involves a team approach including therapists, doctors, and dietitians. Here are some common elements:

- **Psychotherapy:** Individual, group, or family therapy to address underlying emotional issues. Cognitive Behavioral Therapy (CBT) is commonly used to challenge distorted thinking patterns about food and weight.

- **Nutritional Rehabilitation:** Developing healthy eating habits and restoring a healthy weight.
- **Medical Monitoring:** Monitoring for physical complications of the eating disorder.
- **Medications:** In some cases, medications may be used to treat co-occurring conditions like depression or anxiety.

Debunking the Myths: Understanding Feeding and Swallowing Disorders

Feeding and swallowing disorders, also known as dysphagia, can affect people of all ages and abilities. These conditions can make eating and drinking challenging and even dangerous.

Unfortunately, many myths and misconceptions surround dysphagia. Let's explore some common ones to create a clearer understanding:

- **Myth: Dysphagia only affects older adults.**

Reality: While it's more common in older adults due to strokes or neurological conditions, dysphagia can affect people of any age due to various reasons like prematurity, developmental delays, or injuries.

- **Myth: People with dysphagia can't eat or drink anything.**

Reality: Many people with dysphagia can still enjoy food and drinks with modifications. These may include thickened liquids, pureed foods, or specific feeding techniques.

- **Myth: Dysphagia is just about choking.**

Reality: Choking is a risk, but dysphagia can also cause problems like coughing, aspiration (food or liquid entering the lungs), and difficulty swallowing.

- **Myth: People with dysphagia are just picky eaters.**

Reality: Discomfort, anxiety, or physical challenges associated with swallowing can make someone seem picky. It's not about preference, but safety and managing the swallowing process.

- **Myth: Thickened liquids are gross and taste bad.**

Reality: Thickening agents have come a long way, and there are many flavor options available to make thickened liquids more palatable.

- **Myth: Feeding therapy is just about learning to swallow again.**

Reality: Feeding therapy can address various aspects of dysphagia, including strengthening oral muscles, improving coordination, and developing safe swallowing techniques.

- **Myth: There's no point in treating dysphagia in later stages of life.**

Reality: Even if complete recovery isn't possible, therapy can improve a person's quality of life by reducing the risk of aspiration pneumonia and allowing them to enjoy food more safely.

- **Myth: People with feeding tubes can't eat or drink anything by mouth.**

Reality: Feeding tubes are often used for supplemental nutrition, and some individuals with dysphagia may still be able to enjoy some foods and drinks orally with therapy and safe strategies.

- **Myth: Dysphagia is a temporary condition that goes away on its own.**

Reality: While some causes of dysphagia may improve, others are chronic and require ongoing management.

- **Myth: Talking about dysphagia is embarrassing.**

Reality: Open communication between caregivers, healthcare professionals, and the individual with dysphagia is crucial for successful management. There's no shame in seeking help and discussing this condition.

- **Myth: Dysphagia means a person can't enjoy mealtimes anymore.**

Reality: With creativity, planning, and support, people with dysphagia can still experience the social and emotional aspects of mealtimes.

- **Myth: Only doctors and therapists can help with dysphagia.**

Reality: Caregivers and family members play a vital role in supporting safe eating habits and following feeding recommendations.

- **Myth: Children with dysphagia will outgrow it.**

Reality: Early intervention and therapy are crucial for children with dysphagia. While some may improve significantly, others may require ongoing support throughout their lives.

- **Myth: Dysphagia is a sign of weakness or lack of willpower.**

Reality: Dysphagia is a medical condition, not a reflection of a person's strength or determination.

- **Myth: There's no hope for living a fulfilling life with dysphagia.**

Reality: Many people with dysphagia live happy and fulfilling lives. With proper management, support, and a positive attitude, they can still enjoy delicious food, social interaction, and the pleasures associated with mealtimes.

By understanding these myths, we can create a more supportive environment for people with feeding and swallowing disorders.

Dining with Dignity: A Legacy of Inclusion

Swallowing difficulties, or dysphagia, touch millions of lives. While it can present hurdles for your characters, it doesn't have to be a roadblock. This section equips you to create authentic, resilient, and inspiring characters with dysphagia.

Weaving a Tapestry of Rich Representation:

- **Research Makes Real:** Before you write, delve into the world of dysphagia. Understand the spectrum of challenges, from mild difficulty with liquids to dependence on feeding tubes. Research the nuances of different causes so you can tailor your character's experience. Consider consulting with healthcare professionals or support groups for a deeper understanding. Some resources are included below.
- **Beyond the Swallow:** Dysphagia is more than mechanics. Explore the emotional and social impact. Show the frustration of a missed bite, the anxiety of mealtimes, or the isolation that can creep in when sharing food becomes difficult. Consider incorporating coping strategies your characters develop to navigate these challenges.
- Imagine a scene where your character, Sarah, is at a family gathering. A delicious pot roast is served, but Sarah can only manage pureed vegetables due to her dysphagia. Show the internal struggle on Sarah's face as she watches others enjoy the meal. Later, have Sarah confide in a trusted friend about the frustration of missing out on shared flavors and textures.

Strength and Resilience in the Face of Challenges:

Coping Mechanisms: Highlight the ways your character copes. This could involve adaptive utensils, thickened liquids, or practicing compensatory swallowing techniques learned in therapy.

- **A Life Beyond Limitations:** Dysphagia doesn't define a person. Showcase your character's passions, talents, and strengths in other aspects of life. Their love for cooking, for example, might translate into creative ways to adapt recipes or prepare meals for others.
- Show William, a character with dysphagia who loves to cook, researching thickened broths and creative pureed ingredients to modify his favorite recipes. He might find enjoyment in experimenting with flavors and textures to create delicious meals he can still enjoy.

Empowerment Through Advocacy and Support:

- **Self-Advocacy:** Show your character speaking up for themselves. This could involve requesting modifications at restaurants, seeking accessible dining options, or educating others about dysphagia.
- **The Power of Support:** Portray the importance of a strong support system – from healthcare professionals to understanding family and friends.
- For Sarah, who loves food and struggles with dysphagia, becoming an advocate for accessible dining options might be a way to connect with her passion. She could raise awareness about dysphagia and advocate for restaurants to offer modified menus or thicker broths to cater to a wider range of dietary needs.

Breaking Down Barriers for a More Inclusive World:

- **Shattering Stereotypes:** Dysphagia affects people of all ages and backgrounds. Avoid portraying it as a disease of the elderly or the infirm.
- **Inclusive Dining:** Advocate for a world where everyone can enjoy the social and cultural aspects of food. Show accessible dining environments where modifications are welcomed and celebrated.
- Show a family gathering where everyone participates in the meal preparation. Adaptive utensils like weighted forks or specialized cups are readily available for those who need them. The family uses thickened broths for stews and purees vegetables alongside regular dishes, creating a sense of shared enjoyment despite the modifications.

Promoting Understanding: A Shared Journey:

Instead of simply stating the challenges of dysphagia, consider how you can subtly educate your readers through the character's experiences. Weave in details that hint at the difficulties without explicit explanation.

- **Subtle Sensory Details:** Describe a character with dysphagia experiencing a meal. Instead of explicitly stating the challenges, focus on sensory details that subtly hint at the difficulties. Mention the character taking small, controlled bites, savoring the flavors deliberately, or focusing on the sounds of others chewing.
- **Internal Conflict and Decision Making:** Show a character with dysphagia internally debating what to order at a restaurant. Their thought process can reveal the limitations and considerations they face when choosing food, subtly educating readers about the complexities of dining with dysphagia.
- **Character Learning Journey:** Let the character embark on a learning journey about dysphagia. They might attend a support group meeting where other members discuss their experiences and coping mechanisms. Readers can learn alongside the character about different types of

dysphagia and the emotional impact it can have.

- **Doctor's Appointment with Explanations:** Include a scene where the character visits a doctor or speech-language pathologist for a dysphagia evaluation. The healthcare professional can explain the condition, its causes, and potential treatment options in a clear but concise way. This can subtly educate readers without an infodump.
- **Conversations with Family or Friends:** Show the character having conversations with family or friends about their dysphagia. These conversations can highlight the emotional toll of the condition and the importance of communication and support. Readers can learn about the impact dysphagia can have on social interactions.

The Power of Storytelling: Leaving a Legacy of Inclusion

By portraying characters with dysphagia with authenticity, strength, and a desire for inclusion, you can challenge stigma, promote understanding, and inspire both your characters and readers. Dining, after all, should be about connection, not limitation.

This is your Legacy: As authors, we have the power to give voice to those often unheard. Through thoughtful representation, we can empower individuals with dysphagia to claim their rightful place at the table – literally and figuratively. They deserve to be active participants in our stories, just as they deserve a place at society's table.

But the impact goes beyond the page. By educating ourselves and our readers about dysphagia, we contribute to a more inclusive world. We can imagine a future where everyone can experience the joy of food, connection, and shared meals – a future where dining is accessible and enjoyable for all.

Let our stories not only reflect reality but inspire us to create it. Let the final bite be one of understanding, acceptance, and a shared table, where everyone can savor the company and the meal.

For More Information:

- **American Speech-Language Association:** https://www.asha.org/publi c/speech/swallowing/
- **John Hopkins Medicine:** https://www.hopkinsmedicine.org/health/con ditions-and-diseases/swallowing-disorders
- **Mayo Clinic:** https://www.mayoclinic.org/diseases-conditions/dyspha gia/symptoms-causes/syc-20372028
- **National Institute of Neurological Disorders and Stroke:** https://www. ninds.nih.gov/health-information/disorders/swallowing-disorders
- **Cleveland Clinic:** https://my.clevelandclinic.org/health/symptoms/211 95-dysphagia-difficulty-swallowing
- **National Foundation of Swallowing Disorders:** https://swallowingdiso rderfoundation.com/
- **National Dysphagia Diet Standardisation Initiative**: https://iddsi.org/
- **American Board of Swallowing and Swallowing Disorders:** https://ww w.swallowingdisorders.org/page/commonquestions
- **Anatomy and Physiology of Swallowing Video:** https://youtu.be/SBbNx M7g2vg?si=—Gp0i-1sECXKmAP
- **Video explaining dysphagia**: https://youtu.be/oCqryR1526M?si=3OU2 WW29JgofBEMT
- **Video explaining dysphagia**: https://youtu.be/KNYgbN9SIfk?si=dfR381 icep9dayYk
- **Video of Normal vs Abnormal Barium Swallow:** https://youtu.be/fqG0 QmlaFMs?si=SV8VSwtzGOcM-cBZ
- **Video- Swallowing Wellness:** https://youtu.be/83PylXUHZlg?si=MNB Lku9RHI1qBrJR

Character Checklist: Swallowing and Feeding Disorders

This checklist is designed to help you develop a character with a swallowing or feeding disorder in a sensitive and authentic way.

Character Background:

- Specific Disorder (if known): Does your character have dysphagia (swallowing difficulty), oral motor dysfunction, a feeding disorder (e.g., Avoidant/Restrictive Food Intake Disorder - ARFID), or another swallowing/feeding challenge?
- Age of Onset: When did the disorder develop (childhood, adulthood)? Was there a triggering event (e.g., stroke, head injury, illness)?
- When were they diagnosed? Who diagnosed them? What was the professional's attitude toward the disorder? How did they feel about the diagnosis? Were they given advice/recommendations?
- Severity: How severe is the disorder? Does your character require complete tube feeding, a special diet, or thickened liquids?
- Cause (if known): Is there a known cause for the disorder (e.g., neurological condition, muscle weakness, anatomical abnormalities)?

Eating and Swallowing Challenges:

- Swallowing Difficulty: Does your character choke or cough frequently while eating or drinking?
- Oral Motor Skills: Does your character have difficulty chewing, sucking, or moving food in their mouth?
- Sensory Issues: Does your character have sensory sensitivities related to food textures, smells, or tastes?
- Nutritional Needs: How are your character's nutritional needs met (oral intake, tube feeding, supplements)?

Communication and Treatment:

- Self-Monitoring: Is your character aware of their swallowing or feeding difficulties? Do they participate in mealtimes or self-care as much as possible?
- Speech Therapy/Occupational Therapy: Does your character receive

therapy to improve their swallowing or oral motor skills?
- Medical Support: Does your character require assistance from a doctor, nurse, or caregiver during mealtimes?

Emotional Impact:

- Frustration: Does your character experience frustration due to their inability to eat or drink normally?
- Anxiety: Does mealtime cause anxiety or fear of choking?
- Low Self-Esteem: Does the disorder impact your character's self-esteem or body image?
- Social Isolation: Does the disorder limit your character's ability to participate in social meals or outings?
- What do they wish others knew?

Additional Considerations:

- Impact on Daily Life: How does the disorder affect your character's daily routine and independence?
- Support System: Does your character have a supportive family, friends, or caregivers who understand their needs?
- Character Development: How does the swallowing/feeding disorder shape your character's personality, coping mechanisms, and relation-ship with food?

Narrative Choices:

- Sensory Details: How will you describe the character's experience of eating (textures, tastes, anxieties)?
- Internal Monologue: Will you use internal monologue to explore your character's thoughts and feelings about mealtimes?
- Balance: Have you balanced authenticity with the need for clear and engaging storytelling?

Character Development:

- Strengths and Struggles: How does your character's swallowing/feeding disorder impact their daily life and interactions with others?
- Beyond the Disorder: What are your character's strengths and personality traits beyond their eating challenges?
- Avoid Stereotypes: Have you avoided relying solely on the disorder to define your character?
- Choices: Did you give your character choices in treatment and coping strategies?

Representation:

- Respectful Portrayal: Have you portrayed your character's disorder with respect and sensitivity?
- Avoidance of Caricatures: Have you avoided stereotypical or exaggerated representations of people with swallowing or feeding disorders?

Remember:

This checklist is a starting point; not all characters with swallowing/feeding disorders will experience all of these aspects.

- Research the specific disorder to ensure an accurate portrayal.
- Consider including resources for readers who want to learn more.
- Focus on your character's unique strengths, resilience, and approach to mealtimes.

Challenge Accepted: Experiencing Simulated Dysphagia for a Day to Deepen Your Characters

Crafting characters with feeding and swallowing disorders requires a nuanced understanding of the challenges they face. Research is essential, but to truly connect with their struggles, consider this bold proposition: **try simulating dysphagia for a day**.

Understanding Dysphagia

Dysphagia, or swallowing difficulty, can affect people of all ages. It can make eating and drinking challenging and sometimes even dangerous. There are different types of dysphagia, each causing unique challenges.

The Challenge: 24 Hours of Modified Eating and Drinking

For 24 hours, modify your eating and drinking habits to simulate the experience of dysphagia. Here are some ways to achieve this:

- **Thicken Liquids:** Thicken all liquids you consume with thickeners like xanthan gum or cornstarch to mimic the consistency needed for safe swallowing in some cases of dysphagia.
- **Smaller Portions:** Eat small, controlled bites throughout the day, simulating the need to take extra care and time while eating.
- **Modified Utensils:** Use specialized utensils like bent spoons or angled cups that may be helpful for individuals with dysphagia.
- **Focus on Texture:** Pay close attention to the texture of your food, experiencing how certain textures might be difficult or unsafe to swallow.

Why Simulate Dysphagia?

- **Empathy Through Experience:** This challenge isn't meant to mimic a specific medical condition perfectly. It's about understanding the anxiety and frustration associated with eating and drinking, which can be simple actions for most people.
- **Beyond Messy Meals:** Dysphagia is more than just spilling food. This exercise broadens your perspective on how it can impact a character's social interactions and relationship with food.
- **Respectful Representation:** By experiencing the limitations of dysphagia, you gain a deeper appreciation for the specialized diets, feeding techniques, and emotional challenges people with dysphagia manage.

Important Considerations:

- **Safety:** This is a simulation, not a medical treatment. If you have any pre-existing swallowing difficulties, consult a healthcare professional before attempting this challenge.
- **Focus on Alternatives**: Explore alternative sources of nutrition like meal replacement shakes if necessary, mimicking the dietary adjustments people with dysphagia may require.
- **Mindful Eating:** Slow down and pay close attention to the entire process of eating and swallowing, focusing on the sensations and potential challenges.

The Power of Vulnerability

This challenge isn't about replicating a medical condition perfectly. It's about opening yourself up to a new experience. By experiencing the limitations of dysphagia, even for a day, you'll gain a deeper understanding of the characters you create.

This empathy will translate into richer, more authentic portrayals, ensuring your characters with feeding and swallowing disorders are not defined by their limitations, but by their resilience and determination to enjoy the act of eating.

Are you ready to accept the challenge?

10

Speech-Language Pathologist

Your Friendly, Neighborhood Communication Expert

peech-Language Pathologists (SLPs), also known as speech therapists, are the superheroes of communication! They dedicate themselves to helping people of all ages overcome challenges with speaking, understanding language, and swallowing. Here's a breakdown of the journey to becoming an SLP, to enhance the authenticity of characters in your writing:

Education:

- **Undergraduate Preparation:** Bachelor's Degree in Communication Sciences and Disorders requires specialized courses such as Speech Anatomy and Physiology and Phonetics. Solid coursework in areas like biology, linguistics, and psychology prepares students for graduate studies.
- **Master's Degree:** An accredited master's degree in speech-language pathology is the foundation. This program typically takes two years and includes coursework and hands-on clinical experience (around 400 hours working with clients under supervision).

Licensure and Certification:

- **ASHA Certification:** The American Speech-Language-Hearing Association (ASHA) is the gold standard for SLP certification in the US. To earn the prestigious CCC-SLP (Certificate of Clinical Competence in Speech-Language Pathology) designation, aspiring SLPs must:
- **Pass the Praxis Examination** in Speech-Language Pathology (a standardized test).
- **Complete a supervised Clinical Fellowship Year (CF)** of at least 9 months full-time, similar to a physician's residency.
- **State Licensure:** Each state has its own licensure requirements, which usually align with ASHA certification standards. Educational Licensure (for School Settings):
- **Educator Certification:** Most states require SLPs working in schools to obtain an additional teaching license or educational specialist certification. These may involve additional coursework or background checks.

Remember: The path to becoming an SLP takes dedication and passion for communication. By understanding these requirements, you can portray characters who embark on this rewarding career journey.

Scope of Practice

Ever wondered what an SLP can do? Buckle up, because they wear many hats! This section dives into the exciting world of a Speech-Language Pathologist's scope of practice. We'll explore the different areas they assess and treat, from communication delays in children to swallowing difficulties in adults. Here's a breakdown to add depth to your characters who interact with SLPs:

Evaluation Powerhouse:

Imagine a detective kit for communication skills – that's what SLPs use for assessment. They employ various tools:

- **Standardized Tests:** These pre-designed tests measure speech, language, and swallowing abilities and compare it to average abilities.
- **Informal Assessments:** These are customized observations and tasks to get a deeper understanding of an individual's strengths and weaknesses.
- **Speech and Language Samples:** SLPs analyze recordings of natural conversation or specific tasks to identify patterns.
- **Clinical Observations:** Observing how someone communicates in different settings provides valuable insights.
- **Barium Swallow Procedures** (for swallowing disorders): These specialized X-ray tests help SLPs visualize swallowing function.
- **Screenings:** SLPs regularly perform speech, language, swallowing, and hearing screenings.

Treatment Tailored to the Individual:

SLPs work in various settings like schools, clinics, hospitals, and nursing homes. They treat people across the lifespan, from infants to older adults.

Once they understand a client's needs, SLPs create personalized treatment plans. These plans draw on their extensive training and utilize evidence-based therapy techniques to address specific goals:

- **Speech Articulation:** Improving the clarity and accuracy of spoken sounds.
- **Language Comprehension and Expression:** Helping individuals understand and use language effectively.
- **Voice Quality:** Addressing concerns like hoarseness or pitch problems.
- **Fluency:** Managing stuttering or cluttering for smoother speech.
- **Swallowing Function:** Developing strategies for safe and efficient

swallowing.

Therapy in Action:

SLPs conduct therapy sessions individually or in groups, using a variety of engaging approaches:

- **Exercises and Drills:** Practicing specific skills in a structured way.
- **Play-Based Activities (especially for children): Learning through fun and interactive games.**
- **Technology-Assisted Interventions:** Using computer programs or apps to enhance therapy.

Swallowing Specialists:

Some SLPs specialize in swallowing disorders (dysphagia). They assess swallowing function, recommend strategies for safe eating and drinking, and create personalized rehabilitation programs. These might include swallowing exercises to improve muscle coordination.

Teamwork Makes the Dream Work:

SLPs don't work in isolation. Collaboration with other healthcare professionals is key:

- **Physicians:** For medical diagnosis and management of underlying conditions.
- **Audiologists:** For hearing-related concerns that can impact communication.
- **Occupational Therapists:** To address challenges with daily activities related to communication and feeding/swallowing.
- **Psychologists:** To support individuals with emotional aspects of communication disorders.

Spreading Awareness:

SLPs are passionate about promoting communication health. They often participate in community outreach programs:

- **Workshops and Presentations:** Educating professionals about communication development and disorders.
- **Resources for Caregivers and Educators:** Providing tools and information to support individuals with communication challenges.

By understanding the world of SLPs, you can create characters who seek help for communication difficulties and embark on a journey of improvement with the support of these dedicated professionals.

Keeping Up-to-Date: The Lifelong Learning of Speech-Language Pathologists

Speech-Language Pathology is a constantly evolving field. To stay sharp and offer the best possible care, SLPs are dedicated to continuous learning:

Staying on Top of Research:

- **Journals:** They actively seek out the latest research findings in publications like the American Journal of Speech-Language Pathology (AJSLP) or the Journal of Speech, Language, and Hearing Research (JSLHR). This keeps them informed about cutting-edge therapies and best practices.
- **Evidence-Based Approach:** By integrating research findings into their treatment plans, SLPs ensure their interventions are not only effective but also culturally sensitive and appropriate for each client's background.

Continuing Education:

- **Lifelong Learners:** The field of speech-language pathology is constantly evolving, so SLPs are committed to lifelong learning. They participate in ongoing professional development activities such as workshops, conferences, and continuing education courses.
- **National Certification (CCC-SLP):** Maintaining their national certification through the American Speech-Language-Hearing Association (ASHA) requires SLPs to complete at least 30 hours of approved continuing education every three years.
- **State Requirements:** Individual states may have additional continuing education requirements for maintaining state licensure.

Benefits of Continuous Learning:

This commitment to staying current with the latest advancements allows SLPs to:

- **Provide High-Quality Care:** By using the most effective and up-to-date therapies, SLPs can deliver the best possible outcomes for their clients.
- **Adapt to New Challenges:** As research progresses and new communication disorders emerge, continuous learning equips SLPs with the necessary knowledge to address them effectively.
- **Stay Passionate:** Engaging in new learning keeps SLPs passionate about their field and motivated to provide exceptional care.

Adding Depth to Your Characters:

Consider portraying an SLP who incorporates new research findings into their treatment approach. You can also showcase their dedication to attending conferences or workshops to further their expertise.

Myths of the SLP

Myth: Speech pathologists only work with children who stutter.

Reality: Speech-language pathologists (SLPs) work with individuals of all ages, from infants to adults. They address a wide range of communication disorders including stuttering, articulation disorders, language delays/disorders, apraxia of speech, dysphagia (swallowing difficulties), voice disorders, and even social communication challenges associated with autism spectrum disorder.

Myth: Speech pathologists just teach people how to speak properly.

Reality: While improving speech clarity is a part of their work, SLPs use a holistic approach. They assess communication needs, develop individualized treatment plans, utilize various therapeutic techniques, and collaborate with other professionals to ensure overall communication success.

Myth: Anyone can be a speech pathologist, you just need to be good with kids.

Reality: Speech pathology is a rigorous profession requiring a master's degree and state licensure. SLPs undergo extensive coursework in anatomy, physiology, linguistics, and communication disorders, followed by supervised clinical experience.

Myth: Speech therapy is all about drills and exercises.

Reality: While some drills might be used, modern speech therapy is often play-based and engaging for children. For adults, therapy can involve conversation strategies, compensatory techniques, or technology-assisted tools.

Myth: Speech therapy only helps with spoken communication.

Reality: SLPs also work with individuals who use Augmentative and Alternative Communication (AAC) methods to improve their ability to express themselves. AAC can involve picture boards, electronic devices, or other tools to support communication.

Myth: Seeing a speech pathologist is a sign of intelligence problems.

Reality: Communication challenges don't necessarily reflect intelligence. Many factors can contribute to communication difficulties, and early intervention with a speech pathologist can significantly improve outcomes.

Myth: My child will eventually outgrow their communication disorder without therapy.

Reality: While some communication difficulties might resolve naturally, early intervention from a speech pathologist can significantly improve outcomes and prevent long-term struggles.

Myth: Speech therapy is expensive and not covered by insurance.

Reality: Many insurance plans cover speech therapy, especially when medically necessary. Early intervention programs and school-based services can also provide speech therapy at little or no cost.

Myth: Speech pathologists only work in clinics.

Reality: SLPs work in various settings, including:

- Hospitals and rehabilitation centers
- Schools and early intervention programs
- Private practices
- Home healthcare
- Teletherapy settings

Myth: Technology can replace speech therapy.

Reality: While technology can be a valuable tool in speech therapy, it cannot replace the expertise and personalized approach of a qualified speech pathologist.

Myth: Speech pathologists and speech teachers are the same thing.

Reality: Speech-Language Pathologists (SLPs) and speech teachers have distinct roles:

- **Speech-Language Pathologists (SLPs):** As mentioned previously, SLPs are licensed healthcare professionals with a master's degree who diagnose and treat communication disorders across the lifespan. They address a wide range of communication needs, from speech clarity and language development to swallowing difficulties and social communication skills.
- **Speech Teachers:** Speech teachers typically work in educational settings and focus on public speaking skills, vocal techniques, and effective communication strategies for a general audience. While they might provide instruction on articulation or pronunciation, they don't diagnose or treat communication disorders.
- **Speech-Language Pathology Assistant (SLP-A):** SLP-As help a certified speech pathologist with therapy, outreach and administrative tasks under supervision.

For More Information:

- **American Speech-Language Hearing Association:** https://www.asha.org/public/who-are-speech-language-pathologists/
- **U.S. Bureau of Labor Statistics:** https://www.bls.gov/ooh/healthcare/speech-language-pathologists.htm
- **Speech Pathology Graduate Programs.org:** https://www.speechpathologygraduateprograms.org/what-is-speech-language-pathology/

Challenges to Deepen Your Understanding of Speech-Language Pathologists (SLPs)

Crafting characters as SLPs requires more than just knowing their job title. To truly capture their challenges and triumphs, consider these experiences:

Challenge 1: The Detective's Dilemma

Scenario: Roleplay a therapy session with a non-verbal person. Your task is to decipher their needs and wants based on subtle cues like facial expressions, gestures, and body language. This challenge highlights the detective work SLPs do to understand a client's communication intent.

Challenge 2: The Frustration Barrier

Scenario: Attempt to explain a complex concept (e.g., grammar rules, pronunciation techniques) to someone who struggles with those very areas. Experience the frustration of wanting someone to understand, but facing limitations in their learning process. This challenge mirrors the patience and perseverance required of SLPs.

Challenge 3: The Technological Maze

Scenario: Spend a day using various AAC (Augmentative and Alternative Communication) devices. Explore the challenges of navigating unfamiliar interfaces and expressing yourself effectively with limited options. This challenge highlights the importance of SLPs in selecting and training individuals on appropriate AAC tools.

Challenge 4: The Emotional Rollercoaster

Scenario: Shadow an SLP for a day, witnessing their interactions with a diverse group of clients. Experience the spectrum of emotions, from the joy of breakthroughs to the frustration of setbacks. This challenge portrays the emotional intelligence and resilience required of SLPs.

Challenge 5: Listen Like an SLP

Choose Your Focus: Before you start the movie, pick a specific aspect of communication to focus on. Here are some options:

- **Sounds:** Focus on specific sounds like "s," "r," or "l." Notice how clearly or incorrectly different characters pronounce these sounds.
- **Articulation:** Pay attention to how characters move their lips and tongue while speaking. Are there any difficulties forming specific sounds?
- **Verb Tenses:** Track how characters use verb tenses (past, present, future). Do they struggle with using the correct tense or switching tenses appropriately?
- **Sentence Structure:** Listen for complete sentences, sentence fragments, or unusual sentence structures used by characters.
- **Active Listening:** While watching the movie, become an active listener. Don't just follow the plot; pay close attention to the spoken dialogue.
- **Catch and Note:** Whenever you encounter an instance related to your chosen focus area (e.g., mispronounced sound, incorrect verb tense), pause the movie and jot down a quick note.

By experiencing these challenges, you'll gain a deeper appreciation for the dedication, creativity, and expertise of SLPs who empower individuals to overcome communication barriers and find their voice.

11

Sign Language and other Alternative and Augmentative Communication (AAC)

Beyond Words: Exploring Sign Language and AAC in Your Characters

Imagine a world where communication transcends spoken words. A world where gestures, pictures, and even electronic devices become languages themselves, weaving a tapestry of understanding. This is the world of **Augmentative and Alternative Communication (AAC)**, and within this vibrant realm lies a powerful tool: sign language.

Sign language isn't just another way to speak with your hands; it's a complete and complex communication system, often serving as a primary language for individuals who face challenges with spoken language. As writers, we strive to create authentic voices for our characters, and that includes those who express themselves through alternative methods.

This chapter dives deep into the world of AAC, with a particular focus on sign language, empowering you to craft characters who bridge the communication gap through this expressive visual language.

Sign Language: An Integral Part of the AAC Symphony

AAC encompasses a wide range of tools and strategies, and sign language stands out as a cornerstone within this system. Understanding its significance as a form of AAC is crucial. We'll explore how sign language functions as a fully developed language with its own grammar, syntax, and rich vocabulary.

Beyond Words: The Power of Representation

By including characters who use sign language, a vital form of AAC, you open a door to a broader human experience. You challenge stereotypes about communication and create narratives that resonate with a wider audience. This journey begins with appreciating the power of sign language and the diverse populations it empowers.

Exploring the Tapestry of Communication

Get ready to delve into the expressive world of sign language, where hand movements, facial expressions, and body language combine to create a nuanced form of communication. We'll also explore the versatility of other AAC tools and delve into the ever-evolving technology that's changing the way we communicate altogether. Let's weave characters who use AAC, particularly sign language, into the fabric of your stories, celebrating the beautiful symphony of communication in all its forms.

Sign Language: A Language in Motion

Before diving into the world of AAC, let's explore Sign Language, another vital tool for those who experience challenges with spoken language. Often mistaken for simple gestures, Sign Language stands tall as a complete and natural language, brimming with its own grammar, syntax, and a rich vocabulary. This complexity allows for the expression of a full range of ideas and emotions.

Beyond Gestures: A Complex Language of Its Own

Unlike a system of basic gestures used alongside spoken language, Sign Language boasts a complex structure. It utilizes handshapes, facial expressions, body language, and movement in space to weave meaning. Imagine nouns, verbs, adjectives, even tense and negation conveyed through this intricate dance of visual elements. Sign Languages, like spoken languages, have distinct regional variations, dialects, and even slang!

More Than Words: Visuospatial Thinking and Sign Language

This emphasis on visual elements ties into the unique cognitive strengths of Deaf individuals. Sign language fluency is linked to visuospatial thinking, the ability to process information visually and understand spatial relationships. This can lead to advantages in visual memory and tasks like mental rotation.

Accuracy and Cultural Nuances: Bringing Sign Language to Life

Here's your cheat sheet for incorporating Sign Language into your narrative:

- **Research is Key:** American Sign Language (ASL) and British Sign Language (BSL) are entirely different languages, and variations exist within ASL itself. Consult with a Deaf individual or reliable resources to ensure accurate handshapes, facial expressions, and grammar.
- **More Than Hands:** Sign language is a full-body experience. Facial expressions and body language are crucial for conveying meaning. A furrowed brow can indicate frustration, while a raised eyebrow signifies a question. Pay attention to these non-manual elements for a richer portrayal.
- **Cultural Sensitivity:** The Deaf community has a rich and vibrant culture. Avoid stereotypes and portray Deaf characters as multifaceted individ-

uals with dreams and aspirations. Consider the cultural context when depicting social interactions involving sign language.

· **Accessibility and Technology:** The world is becoming increasingly accessible for sign language users. Technology is playing a significant role, with the development of sign language recognition software, video interpreting services, and mobile apps for learning signs.

Now, let's delve into the world of Augmentative and Alternative Communication (AAC).

Cracking the Communication Code: A Guide to AAC

Imagine a world where communication isn't confined to spoken words. Gestures, facial expressions, pictures, and even technology can all weave a tapestry of understanding. This is the world of Augmentative and Alternative Communication (AAC), and it offers a lifeline to those who find spoken language challenging.

Beyond Speech Therapy

Think about a child with Apraxia who struggles to form words. They might use pictures of familiar objects on a communication board to request a snack or a favorite toy. Or perhaps an adult who has difficulty using spoken communication after a stroke now relies on a voice-generating device to express complex thoughts and feelings. These are all valid forms of AAC, empowering individuals to connect with the world around them.

The AAC Toolbox

The world of AAC (Augmentative and Alternative Communication) offers a vast array of tools to support individuals with communication challenges. Broadly, AAC can be categorized into two main groups: unaided AAC and aided AAC.

Even in everyday interactions, most individuals use a combination of spoken language, gestures, facial expressions, and even tone of voice to convey meaning. This is known as multimodal communication. AAC builds on these natural communication skills to provide a wider range of tools for those who face challenges with spoken language.

Choosing the Right AAC:

Before exploring specific AAC tools, it's crucial to consider the unique needs of each individual. Here are some key factors to consider when making AAC decisions:

- **Individual Abilities:** A person's physical abilities, such as fine motor skills, vision, and hearing, will influence the type of aided AAC (low-tech or high-tech) that might be most suitable. **Additionally, intellectual capabilities and language level are important factors.** Someone with strong cognitive skills might benefit from a more complex AAC system with features for vocabulary building and sentence construction. Conversely, someone with a lower language level might need a simpler system with fewer options to avoid overwhelming them.
- **Communication Needs:** Evaluate the level of complexity required for communication. Unaided AAC might be sufficient for basic needs, while aided AAC with more elaborate options might be necessary for expressing complex thoughts and ideas. Consider the individual's intellectual abilities and language level here as well. Someone with a higher language level might need an AAC system that allows for more nuanced expression.
- **Personal Preferences:** Whenever possible, involve the individual in the decision-making process. Consider their age, interests, and what kind of communication tool they feel most comfortable using.

Unaided AAC:

Unaided AAC is like a built-in communication system we all have. It refers to methods that don't require any external tools. Gestures, facial expressions, body language, and even eye gaze can all be powerful tools for conveying meaning. A child pointing excitedly at a swing or someone using American Sign Language (ASL) are both examples of unaided AAC in action. While these systems may have limitations in universality, they are readily available and can be a crucial starting point for communication.

Aided AAC:

This category offers a wider range of tools and technologies to assist with communication. Low-tech options include communication boards with pictures or symbols, which individuals can point to or use with a scanning device. Think of a laminated board with pictures of food – a person can point to the picture of a sandwich to indicate they're hungry.

High-tech options include voice-generating devices that allow individuals to select words and phrases displayed on a screen, which are then synthesized into speech. These devices can even offer options for environmental control, allowing individuals to operate lights or appliances through their AAC system.

By incorporating characters who use AAC into your narratives, you open a door to a broader spectrum of human experience. You challenge misconceptions about communication and create stories that resonate with a wider audience.

The next sections will delve deeper into the different types of AAC tools and how to portray characters who use them authentically.

Who Needs a Voice? A Look at AAC Users

Augmentative and Alternative Communication (AAC) isn't a one-size-fits-all solution. It empowers a wide range of individuals with complex communication needs. Let's meet some of the people who benefit from AAC:

- **Children with Developmental Delays:** Imagine a child with Down syndrome who struggles to form clear words. AAC provides them with a voice – perhaps through pictures on a communication board or an app with simple phrases. This allows them to express their wants and needs, fostering independence and participation in daily activities.
- **Adults with Acquired Disabilities:** A stroke or ALS can leave someone without their spoken voice. AAC allows them to regain a sense of connection. They might use a voice-generating device to express complex thoughts and feelings, or rely on simpler tools like picture boards.
- **Children with Childhood Apraxia of Speech (CAS):** CAS makes it hard to coordinate the muscles needed for speech. A child with CAS might understand language perfectly, but forming words is a challenge. AAC offers alternative communication pathways, bypassing the physical limitations of speech production.
- **People with Hearing Loss:** Hearing loss can make it difficult to understand spoken language, creating a communication barrier. AAC bridges this gap. Individuals with hearing loss might use pictures, symbols, or even text-based AAC systems to express themselves and participate in conversations, promoting social interaction and inclusion. AAC is an alternative or addition to Sign Language.
- **Others with Complex Communication Needs:** Temporary voice loss due to illness, severe apraxia, or non-verbal autism are all situations where AAC can be beneficial.

The need for AAC is as diverse as the individuals who use it. Some people rely solely on unaided AAC like gestures or sign language. Others use a combination of aided AAC tools (like communication boards or electronic devices) and unaided methods. The specific tools and strategies will depend on the individual's unique needs and communication style.

In the next section, we'll delve deeper into the different types of AAC tools and how to create authentic characters who use them.

Bridging the Gap: How AAC Makes Communication Possible

Imagine a world where communication isn't limited to spoken words. Augmentative and Alternative Communication (AAC) unlocks this world for people who face challenges with traditional speech. It's a communication bridge, empowering them to express themselves and participate actively in life. Let's explore the mechanics of this bridge.

Building the Bridge: Symbols and Selection

At the heart of AAC lies a system of symbols or words that represent messages. These symbols can be anything from pictures on a communication board to written words on a screen. The way a person chooses these symbols depends on their needs and abilities:

- **Direct Selection:** For those with good motor skills, it's like pointing at something you want in a store. They simply touch the desired symbol on a board or screen for immediate communication.
- **Scanning:** For individuals with limited motor skills, scanning offers an alternative. The AAC system highlights rows or columns of symbols one by one, controlled by the user with a switch or joystick, or even eye gaze. When the desired symbol is highlighted, they select it, and their message is conveyed. Think of it like a spotlight finding just the right word.

Crossing the Bridge: Different Outputs for Different Needs

Once a symbol or word is chosen, the AAC system brings the message to life! The output can take various forms:

- **Speech-Generating Devices (SGDs):** These are the voices for people with limited or no spoken language. They convert chosen words or phrases into synthesized speech, allowing verbal communication despite physical limitations. Imagine a device that speaks for you!
- **Text Output:** Some AAC systems prioritize written communication. These devices display the chosen symbols or words on a screen, allowing the user to communicate through text. This is perfect for those comfortable with reading and writing, or for situations where speaking might be difficult.
- **A Multifaceted Approach:** Many AAC systems offer both speech and text output, providing flexibility. People can choose spoken communication for casual interactions and written communication for formal settings or noisy environments.

By understanding how AAC works, you can create characters who use it authentically. The next section will delve into the different types of AAC tools and how to portray them in your stories.

Debunking the Myths: Understanding Sign Language and AAC

Sign language and Augmentative and Alternative Communication (AAC) are vital tools for people who experience challenges with spoken language. Despite their growing presence, many misconceptions surround them. Let's explore common myths to create a clearer understanding:

Sign Language Considerations

- **Myth: Sign language is universal.**

Reality: Just like spoken languages, sign languages have regional variations and distinct grammar. American Sign Language (ASL) is different from British Sign Language (BSL), for example.

- **Myth: Sign language is simply miming.**

Reality: Sign languages are complex with their own grammar, syntax, and vocabulary. They are complete and natural languages, not just gestures.

- **Myth: People who use sign language can't speak or understand spoken language.**

Reality: Many sign language users are bilingual, communicating effectively in both sign language and spoken language (if able).

- **Myth: Learning sign language is too difficult.**

Reality: Like any language, sign language requires dedication and practice, but it can be learned by people of all ages and backgrounds. There are many resources available to facilitate learning.

- **Myth: Sign language is not a "real" language because it's not spoken.**

Reality: Sign languages are fully realized languages with their own structure and complexity. They are just not spoken languages.

- **Myth: All Deaf people use sign language.**

Reality: Sign Language is only one alternative way to communicate. Individuals choose the way they communicate based on many different factors, including ease of learning, ease of use, universality, and dexterity. Often individuals use more than one way of communicating.

AAC Myths:

- **Myth: AAC is only for people who can't speak at all.**

Reality: AAC can be a valuable tool for anyone with communication challenges, regardless of their ability to speak. It can supplement or support spoken language.

- **Myth: AAC is only low-tech picture boards.**

Reality: AAC encompasses a wide range of tools, from low-tech picture boards and communication books to high-tech speech-generating devices with electronic symbols and synthesized speech.

- **Myth: AAC is a replacement for spoken language.**

Reality: The goal of AAC is to augment or support communication, not replace spoken language entirely. Many people who use AAC may also use some spoken language.

- **Myth: People who use AAC are not intelligent.**

Reality: Communication challenges do not reflect intelligence. AAC empowers individuals to express themselves effectively despite their limitations.

- **Myth: Using AAC will make a person lazy and stop trying to speak.**

Reality: AAC is a tool to bridge the communication gap. It doesn't discourage spoken language development when possible.

Sign Language & AAC Together:

- **Myth: Sign language and AAC are interchangeable.**

Reality: Sign language is a complete language, while AAC can encompass various tools. The choice between them depends on the individual's needs and preferences.

- **Myth: Children who use AAC won't learn sign language.**

Reality: Some children may benefit from both sign language and AAC. They can be complementary communication methods.

- **Myth: Only professionals can teach sign language and AAC.**

Reality: There are many resources available for parents, caregivers, and educators to learn the basics of sign language and AAC to support communication. The more rich the input of language, the better the individual will learn language skills.

- **Myth: Using sign language or AAC with a child will delay their spoken language development.**

Reality: Research suggests that exposure to multiple communication methods can actually benefit language development in some cases.

- **Myth: Sign language and AAC isolate people who don't use them.**

Reality: By understanding and respecting these communication methods, we can create a more inclusive environment where everyone can participate meaningfully.

By debunking these myths, we can promote better understanding and create a more inclusive world for people who rely on sign language and AAC to communicate effectively.

Breathing Life into Your Characters: Portraying AAC with Authenticity

We've explored the mechanics of AAC, but how do we translate that into characters who feel real? This section dives into the art of portraying AAC users authentically, moving beyond function to capture the richness of their inner lives and communication styles.

Ditch the Stereotypes, Embrace the Individual

First things first: AAC users are a diverse bunch. They come from all walks of life, with unique personalities and communication preferences.

Resist the urge to portray them as one-dimensional figures – either defined solely by their disability or miraculously overcoming limitations with technology. Instead, focus on who they are – their dreams, quirks, and aspirations. They're the hero on their own journey, and AAC is just one of the tools they use to navigate the world.

Beyond Words: Time, Frustration, and Resilience

Let's be honest, AAC can be slower than spoken conversation or Sign Language. Selecting symbols, navigating menus, and waiting for the device to speak can be frustrating for everyone involved. Incorporate these realities into your narrative.

Show how your character might take extra time to express themselves, or experience glitches that test their patience. This adds depth and authenticity, highlighting their determination to be heard.

A Spectrum of Emotions: Liberation and Self-Discovery

For some characters, AAC is a lifeline. It empowers them to express themselves and connect with the world in ways they never could before. Show the joy of newfound independence and the freedom that comes with clear communication. Explore the positive impact of AAC on their lives.

However, AAC can also be a source of complex emotions. The reliance on technology can be frustrating, and some characters might grapple with feelings of self-consciousness or even shame. Delve into this emotional complexity. Show how using AAC can be a journey of self-discovery and acceptance.

Building Bridges: The Power of Inclusive Interactions

Communication is a two-way street. When writing about AAC users, consider the role their communication partners play. Maybe it's a friend offering extra time to express themselves, a family member patiently helping navigate their AAC system, or simply someone practicing active listening.

Show how characters using AAC can build strong connections and friendships with supportive partners who understand their communication needs. By depicting these positive interactions, you can celebrate the power of inclusivity and the importance of building bridges across communication styles.

Remember, AAC is a tool. The real magic lies in the person using it. By portraying characters with authenticity and nuance, you can challenge stereotypes, foster empathy, and create characters who inspire us all.

Beyond Sign Language: A Spectrum of Choices

Sign language isn't a one-size-fits-all solution. While powerful and expressive, it's not the only option for those with communication challenges. Some individuals might choose alternative communication methods based on personal preference, dexterity limitations, or technological advancements.

Speech therapy and auditory implants can help some improve spoken and auditory comprehension. Others might utilize Cued Speech, a system of handshapes that complements lipreading.

Technological advancements like real-time captioning and voice recognition software offer additional communication pathways. Ultimately, the communication method depends on individual needs, comfort level, and the specific situation.

Celebrating the Beauty of Sign Language

By portraying sign language accurately and with sensitivity, you have the power to showcase its beauty and strength. You can depict characters who use sign language as confident, expressive individuals who communicate effectively and engage in rich social interactions.

Furthermore, you can challenge misconceptions about deafness and promote a more inclusive understanding of communication. Imagine a scene where a character uses sign language to tell a captivating story, their hands painting pictures in the air, their expressions adding layers of meaning.

This portrayal not only advances the plot but also celebrates the vibrancy and power of sign language as a complete and natural language.

Example Dialogues

The following examples showcase how individuals with varying AAC needs can utilize different communication methods in real-life scenarios. We'll see how AAC can empower them to express themselves effectively and engage in meaningful interactions.

Sign Language

Maya hurried into the bustling coffee shop, the aroma of freshly brewed coffee a warm welcome. She spotted her friend, Alex, hunched over a laptop at a corner table, his brow furrowed in concentration. Beside him sat a young woman with bright red hair, her hands moving rapidly in sign language, a frustrated expression on her face.

"Morning, Alex," Maya signed, her hands forming a greeting. "What's the story?"

Alex glanced up, a relieved smile spreading across his face. He signed back, "Sarah here just arrived from California and wants to try that new lavender latte they have. But the barista isn't quite understanding her order."

Sarah, catching the gist of the conversation, signed towards Maya, "They keep asking me what kind of milk I want, but I can't seem to explain I want oat milk with a splash of vanilla syrup."

Understanding dawned on Maya. She signed back to Sarah, a mischievous glint in her eyes, "Leave it to me. I know just the barista who speaks fluent ASL latte art."

Moments later, Maya returned with two steaming mugs, their surfaces adorned with intricate latte art designs. Sarah's face lit up with delight, and she signed her thanks to Maya. The conversation continued in a flurry of hand gestures, filled with laughter and shared stories.

Multimodal AAC, including a Picture Communication App, Text to Speech and Gestures (Apraxia of Speech):

Maya gripped the coffee cup a little too tightly, the warmth seeping into her palm. Noah, across from her, was mid-sentence, a question about drama club dangling in the air. She loved drama club, the thrill of inhabiting another skin, the freedom of expressing emotions that felt tangled in her own throat. But forming the words, that was the battle.

Instead of reaching for her tablet right away, Maya forced a small smile and tried. "Drama..." The word sputtered out, halting and breathless. Noah's eyebrows furrowed slightly, but he didn't interrupt. She squeezed her eyes shut, willing her tongue to cooperate, but another strangled sound was all that emerged. Defeat coiled in her stomach.

Taking a deep breath, Maya reached for her tablet, the familiar gesture a source of comfort. But before she did, she raised a hand, palm open, towards Noah – a silent "wait" to give herself a moment. Her finger tapped a vibrant image - a stage bathed in warm light, silhouettes of actors gesturing wildly. A synthesized voice, slightly robotic but undeniably hers, filled the space: "Drama club was amazing!"

Relief washed over her as Noah grinned, his eyes crinkling at the corners. "Ooo, intense! Are you playing Juliet?"

The corner of Maya's mouth twitched. She tapped another image, a crown sparkling against a black background. The voice spoke again: "Queen this time." She glanced up at Noah, a playful glint in her eye, then raised her hand in a sweeping gesture, a silent portrayal of a regal figure. She typed quickly, adding, "Big lines, exciting!"

Noah chuckled, a warm sound that always managed to relax the knot in her chest. "Of course, the dramatic role," he teased. "Sounds perfect for you, Maya."

Just then, the frustration bubbled up. The damn coffee lid. Her fingers fumbled, the plastic refusing to budge. Before she could clench her hand further, a shadow fell across the table. Noah reached over, his touch light but firm, and twisted the lid free.

A wave of gratitude washed over her. Sometimes, the simplest things became her Everest. She quickly typed a message, the familiar clicks of the virtual keyboard a comforting rhythm. "Thanks." A small icon of a thumbs up appeared on the screen next to the text.

The corner of his lips lifted as he read the message on the screen. "No problem at all." His gaze flickered to the cafe window, sunlight glinting off the gold lettering: "Open Studio: Watercolors for Beginners." "So, anything exciting planned for the weekend?"

Hope sparked in Maya's chest. She tapped furiously, a picture of a paintbrush swirling through a rainbow of colors blossoming on the screen. "Watercolor class Saturday! Trying it out. Wanna join?"

Noah's eyes lit up. "That sounds awesome! Maybe you can paint a scene from your play?"

A smile, genuine and wide, spread across Maya's face. She typed again, the message a silent victory cry: "Great idea! You coming?"

Noah leaned forward, his enthusiasm mirroring her own. "Absolutely! Wouldn't miss it for the world."

The conversation flowed from there, a comfortable blend of typed messages, the occasional synthesized voice, and the silent language of smiles, shared laughter, and Maya's expressive gestures that bridged the gap in spoken communication. In that moment, the world felt a little brighter, the words a little less tangled, and the colors waiting to be captured on a canvas a thrilling promise.

Multimodal AAC - Picture, Signed Words and Speech (phonological disorder)

Lily, a whirlwind of energy in a pigtailed package, burst into the kitchen, a colorful card clutched triumphantly in her hand. She squeezed her eyes shut and pushed out a sound that wobbled between a "j" and a "w." Frustration clouded her face for a moment, then she thrust the card towards Sarah, her mom.

Sarah looked up from chopping vegetables, her smile softening as she recognized the picture card – a cheerful scene of a child holding a glass of orange juice under a bright sun.

"zu–...?" Lily tried again, the word emerging breathy and fragmented. She signed the word for "juice," her little hand twisting and turning in the air with practiced ease.

"Orange juice sounds perfect!" Sarah said, gently taking the card and holding it up for Lily. "You must be thirsty after playing outside."

Lily, unable to contain her excitement, bounced on the balls of her feet and nodded vigorously. She pointed excitedly at the picture on the card, then opened her mouth again. This time, a jumble of sounds emerged, unintelligible but filled with urgency.

Sarah, used to deciphering Lily's unique way of communicating, smiled warmly. "Hot outside, wasn't it?" she guessed, reaching for the refrigerator.

Lily's face lit up. "Ho!" she exclaimed, the single word a burst of triumph.

As Sarah poured the cool, orange liquid into a cup decorated with a big, friendly smiley face, Lily watched intently. Once filled, Sarah handed the cup to her daughter.

Lily, unable to wait any longer, took a generous gulp of the juice, a satisfied sigh escaping her lips. Her eyes darted to the picture on the cup, and a single, clear word tumbled out: "my–ee!"

Sarah couldn't help but laugh. "Yes, smiley face!" she agreed. "Do you want to take another picture outside after you finish your juice?

We can see if we can find something else smiley, like a flower!"

Lily's face lit up. She signed for "yes" with a flourish, and a single, excited word escaped her lips: "Fowuh!"

The kitchen echoed with a melody of sounds – the clinking of Lily's cup, the rustle of the picture card, and the smattering of words and signs – a beautiful symphony that, to Sarah's ears, was music to her heart.

The Symphony of Communication: A Final Act

Our journey through Augmentative and Alternative Communication (AAC) has unveiled a world where possibility dances with innovation. We've explored the heart of AAC, from selecting symbols to the magic of transforming those choices into messages. We've met individuals who benefit from AAC, each with a unique voice and story waiting to be heard.

As writers, we have the power to weave these voices into the fabric of our narratives. By stepping away from stereotypes and embracing authenticity, we can challenge assumptions about communication and celebrate the vast spectrum of human expression.

Imagine characters who use AAC – individuals who laugh, dream, and express themselves with vibrant passion. Their inclusion isn't just about ticking a diversity box; it's about enriching your story and fostering empathy in your readers.

In the end, understanding and portraying AAC is about applauding the symphony of communication. It's a celebration of the diverse ways we connect, a melody that transcends spoken words.

By incorporating AAC into your writing, you have the potential to create a world that's not only entertaining but also inclusive and inspiring. So go forth, writer, and let the characters who use AAC take center stage in your stories. Their voices are waiting to be heard.

For More Information

- **USSAAC** - https://ussaac.org/
- **AAC Institute** - https://aacinstitute.org/
- **Everyone Communicates.org:** http://everyonecommunicates.org/index .html
- **Augmentative and Alternative Communication Camp** - https://youtu.b e/8zuNsuHPRbY?si=eW8utlWy-9Gkcg46
- **AAC: Augmentative & Alternative Communication:** https://youtu.be/ C7GSgpjOwfI?si=hNeoAwRaU6bbWHQf
- **National Institute of Deafness and Other Communication Disorders** - https://www.nidcd.nih.gov/health/assistive-devices-people-hearing-voice-speech-or-language-disorders
- **American Speech-Language Hearing Association** - https://www.asha. org/njc/aac/
- **TEDxMacatawa - Chris Klein - seeing unique abilities** (communicates using AAC device with foot): https://youtu.be/3H3e2MXV6iY?si=IIDVo kTo9L3_2CcG
- **Assistive Technology in Action - Meet Elle:** https://youtu.be/g95TO2 ohnmo?si=0yyRa737SGW-FuVV
- **Pragmatic Language Using ASL in Early Childhood Education:** https://y outu.be/bDFxr6dMJUE?si=sl9Nhfi8tmkbmlyw
- **What is AAC?** https://youtu.be/r3m8_YmTDDM?si=9V9grsSf8JnY6IUK
- **Augmentative and Alternative Devices:** https://youtu.be/Y4ZPJ6a7fXw? si=QdQtKnmCmwd6eiWz
- **ASL as an AAC System:** https://youtu.be/_JW5nEBXcac?si=ny7T_knXH zIUc6na
- **PECS vs AAC vs ASL:** https://youtu.be/QiRhS9AoNwA?si=k8bW2Ams7U 8oHIjB
- **Mainstream vs Deaf School:** https://youtu.be/Xe3EyubGKQo?si=MMgy yxXSaEwiURwq

Character Checklist: Sign Language and AAC Users

Character Background

- **Communication Method:** Sign Language, AAC, or both? Explored other methods before settling?
- **Age at Onset:** Childhood, adulthood? Triggering event (illness, injury)?
- **Diagnosis & Support:** When/by whom? Professional's attitude? Character's reaction? Advice/recommendations given?
- **Cause (if known):** Deafness, speech disorder, developmental delay, etc.?
- **Fluency Level:** How proficient in their chosen method (Sign Language/AAC system)?

Language and Communication

- **Sign Language User:** Specific variety (ASL, BSL)? Fingerspelling or Signed English?
- **AAC User:** Type of system (picture board, electronic device)? Access method (eye gaze, touch)?
- **Receptive Skills:** How well do they understand spoken language?
- **Expressive Skills:** How effectively can they express themselves using their chosen method?

Social Interaction

- **Confidence Level:** Comfort communicating with Sign Language/AAC in various settings?
- **Frustration:** Do they experience frustration due to communication barriers or AAC system limitations?
- **Self-Advocacy:** Do they advocate for their communication needs and preferred methods?
- **Support System:** Do they have a supportive network who understands their communication style?

Character Development

- **Personality:** How does using Sign Language/AAC influence their personality and self-expression?
- **Strengths & Challenges:** How does it impact their daily life and interactions?
- **Beyond Communication:** Strengths, interests, and personality traits beyond their communication method.
- **What They Wish Others Knew:** What does your Character wish others knew about them or their struggles?
- **Choices**: Did you give your character choices about their communication mode or coping strategies?

Narrative Choices

- **Sign Language:** Visually depict sign language use (descriptions, italics for signs)? Consider sensitivity reader for actual signs.
- **AAC:** Describe their use of the system or focus on internal thoughts/desires?
- **Balance:** Balanced portrayal of communication challenges with a clear and engaging story?

Representation

- **Respectful Portrayal:** Respectful and sensitive portrayal of Sign Language/AAC use?
- **Avoiding Stereotypes:** Avoided stereotypical assumptions about Sign Language/AAC users?

Remember

- Starting point - not all experiences will be the same.
- Research specific Sign Languages or AAC systems for accurate portrayal.
- Consider resources for readers who want to learn more.
- Focus on their unique voice, resilience, and communication style.

Challenge Accepted: Stepping into a World of AAC for a Day to Deepen Your Characters

Crafting characters who rely on Augmentative and Alternative Communication (AAC) requires a deep understanding of their unique experiences. Research is valuable, but to truly connect with their world, consider this challenge: spend a day using a simulated AAC system to communicate.

Understanding AAC

AAC empowers individuals with limited or no spoken language to communicate effectively. There are various AAC systems, from low-tech picture boards to high-tech speech-generating devices.

The Challenge: 24 Hours of Simulated AAC

Limit communication to a simulated AAC system for 24 hours. Here are some ways to achieve this:

- **Create a Low-Tech AAC System:** Develop a picture board with common words and phrases you'll need throughout the day.
- **Utilize a Mobile AAC App:** Download a free AAC app and explore its functionalities to experience the limitations and possibilities of a speech-generating device.
- **Partner Up:** Involve a friend or family member who will act as your "communication assistant," helping you navigate conversations and

interpret your selections on the AAC system.

· **Limited Verbal Communication:** Minimize spoken communication as much possible, relying solely on your simulated AAC system for most interactions.

Why Simulate AAC?

· **Empathy Through Experience:** This challenge isn't about mimicking a specific disability. It's about understanding the frustration of limited spoken language and the power of alternative communication methods.
· **Beyond Pointing:** AAC goes beyond simple picture boards. This exercise broadens your perspective on how technology and creativity can empower communication.
· **Respectful Representation:** By experiencing the limitations and potential of AAC, you gain a deeper respect for the resilience and ingenuity of people who rely on these systems to communicate effectively.

Important Considerations:

· **Patience is Key:** Using AAC takes time and practice. Be patient with yourself and those interacting with you.
· **Frustration is Expected:** This experience might be frustrating, especially when expressing complex ideas. Remember, the goal is to gain understanding, not mastery.
· **Focus on Intent:** Despite the limitations, strive to communicate your needs and ideas clearly using your chosen AAC system.

The Power of Vulnerability

This challenge isn't about replicating a disability perfectly. It's about opening yourself up to a new reality. By experiencing the limitations and potential of AAC, even for a day, you'll gain a deeper understanding of the characters you create. This empathy will translate into richer, more authentic portrayals, ensuring your characters who rely on AAC are not defined by their communication method, but by their strength, determination, and unique voice.

Are you ready to accept the challenge?

12

Research and Sensitivity

Respectful Representation: Researching Speech, Hearing & Language Disorders

Speech, hearing, and language disorders (SHALDs) encompass a rich tapestry of human experience. As writers, we have the responsibility to portray these complexities with authenticity and respect. Here's where meticulous research becomes the key to unlocking believable characters with SHALDs.

Understanding the Nuances:

- **Dive Deeper:** SHALDs are a diverse bunch. **Each disorder has its own fingerprint:** unique characteristics, causes, and variations in severity. Invest time in understanding the specific disorder your character has.
- **Manifestations Matter:** Don't settle for textbook definitions. Research **how the chosen disorder plays out in daily life**. Explore the challenges your character might face with speaking, listening, understanding, or expressing language.

Celebrating Individuality:

- **Varied Experiences:** SHALDs affect people in unique ways. **Age of onset, severity, and coping mechanisms** all influence an individual's journey. Avoid a one-size-fits-all narrative – embrace the beautiful spectrum of experiences.

Crafting Authenticity:

- **Firsthand Accounts:** Seek out the voices of those with SHALDs or consult with **speech-language pathologists (SLPs)**. Their insights can be gold, adding invaluable authenticity to your portrayal.

Moving Beyond Stereotypes:

- **Challenge Misconceptions:** SHALDs do not define a person's worth. Dispel stereotypes – a stutter isn't synonymous with nervousness, and aphasia doesn't equate to a lack of intelligence.

Language and Communication:

- **Realistic Patterns:** SHALDs often impact **how people use language**. Research the specific ways the chosen disorder affects speech patterns, vocabulary use, or sentence structure.
- **Adaptive Strategies:** People with SHALDs often develop creative communication tools. Showcasing these **coping mechanisms** adds depth and authenticity to your character.

Through comprehensive research, you gain the power to create characters who are genuine, relatable, and defy misconceptions. Remember, your dedication to authenticity fosters empathy and understanding not only in your readers but also in society as a whole. By portraying SHALDs with respect, you celebrate the beautiful diversity of human communication.

Unveiling the Spectrum: Researching Speech and Language Disorders

Speech and language disorders (SLDs) paint a vibrant but complex picture of human communication. As writers, we have the responsibility to portray these realities with accuracy and sensitivity. But where do we begin?

This guide will equip you to navigate the world of SLD research.

Building Authentic Characters with Speech, Language, and Learning Disorders (SLDs)

Building a Strong Foundation: Reliable Sources

- **Academic Journals:** Unearth deep dives into specific SLDs, causes, and treatments through peer-reviewed research published by respected institutions.
- **Books by Speech-Language Pathologists (SLPs):** Gain a unique perspective from healthcare professionals who work directly with individuals with SLDs.
- **Professional Organizations:** Websites of organizations like the American Speech-Language-Hearing Association (ASHA) serve as treasure troves of reliable information on SLDs, treatment options, and advocacy resources.

Exploring the Digital Wild West (Cautiously):

- **Online Resources:** The internet provides an ocean of information, but navigate cautiously! Seek out websites affiliated with recognized institutions, universities, or healthcare organizations. Always check author credentials and ensure the information is current and evidence-based.

Going Beyond Textbooks: Consulting the Experts

- **Collaboration with SLPs:** Partnering with a licensed SLP can yield invaluable insights on specific disorders, communication strategies used by individuals with SLDs, and the realistic challenges they face.
- **Psychologists and Medical Professionals:** For SLDs with a neurological or psychological component, consulting psychologists or relevant medical professionals can offer a more holistic understanding.

The Power of Lived Experience:

- **Seeking Perspectives:** Connecting with individuals who have SLDs, or with caregivers, provides a unique window into the daily realities and challenges of these disorders. Look for opportunities to interview them or participate in relevant support groups (with permission, of course).

Remember:

- **Ethical Practices:** Always obtain informed consent before interviewing individuals with SLDs. Respect their privacy and ensure anonymity if requested.
- **Cross-referencing:** Don't rely on a single source. Verify information across different credible resources to ensure accuracy and comprehensiveness.
- **Diverse Representation:** Strive to showcase a spectrum of communication challenges faced by individuals, avoiding over-representation of low-incidence disorders in your characters.

Bonus Resource: Statistics on Communication Disorders:
https://www.nidcd.nih.gov/health/statistics

By combining research from reputable sources, collaborating with experts, and seeking perspectives from those with lived experience, you gain a nuanced understanding of SLDs. This knowledge empowers you to craft characters who are not just believable but also inspire empathy and understanding in your readers.

Remember, your dedication to authenticity celebrates the beautiful diversity of human communication.

Crafting Characters with SHALDs: Empathy, Authenticity, and Respect

Speech, hearing, and language disorders (SHALDs) are more than medical terms – they touch every aspect of a person's life. As writers, we have the power to depict these experiences with empathy and respect, fostering a deeper understanding in our readers. Here's how to craft characters with SHALDs in a way that's both sensitive and empowering.

Seeing the World Through Their Eyes:

- **Empathy is the Compass: Step into their shoes.** Consider the frustrations, anxieties, and social challenges your character might face. How does their SHALD impact their self-esteem and confidence?
- **Beyond the Medical Chart:** Explore the **emotional landscape** of SHALDs. Delve into the feelings of isolation, the fear of misunderstanding, or the grief over lost abilities.

Choosing Words with Care:

- **Striking Out Stigma:** Be mindful of the language you use. Avoid outdated or insensitive terms. Organizations like ASHA offer resources on current and respectful terminology. (https://www.asha.org/)
- **Myth Busters:** SHALDs don't define a person's intelligence or worth. Dispel stereotypes – a stutter isn't synonymous with nervousness, and aphasia doesn't mean someone lacks cognitive ability.

Respectful Representation:

Individuals with SHALDs deserve to be portrayed with dignity. Focus on their strengths, passions, and unique perspectives, not just their communication challenges. Accuracy Matters: Research and depict how SHALDs manifest in speech, language use, or listening comprehension. Avoid exaggerated portrayals or resorting to clichés.

Finding Your Allies

To ensure your portrayal is sensitive and authentic, consider collaborating with disability consultants and sensitivity readers who specialize in SHALDs. Disability consultants can provide expert insights into the specific disorder you're depicting, while sensitivity readers can offer feedback on your character's portrayal and identify any potential stereotypes.

Finding Disability Consultants and Sensitivity Readers

When crafting characters with disabilities, including those with Speech, Language, and Hearing Disorders (SHALDs), collaboration with disability consultants and sensitivity readers can elevate your work by ensuring authenticity and avoiding stereotypes. Here are some resources to help you find the right experts:

Disability Consultants:

- **Disability Organizations:** Many disability-focused organizations maintain lists of consultants who specialize in various areas. Look for organizations related to the specific SHALD you're depicting.
- For example, The American Speech-Language-Hearing Association (ASHA) (https://asha.org/) offers a directory of professionals.
- **National Disability Navigator:** This online resource (https://www.ndn.org/) from the National Council on Independent Living (NCIL) can connect you with disability professionals across the US.
- **Social Media:** Look for disability rights advocates and consultants on platforms like Twitter. Use relevant hashtags to find them (e.g., #DisabilityConsultant, #SHALDConsultant).

Sensitivity Readers:

- **Writer's Digest:** This online resource offers a comprehensive article on finding sensitivity readers, including directories and freelance platforms. https://www.writersdigest.com/getting-published/writing-with-intention-on-hiring-a-sensitivity-reader
- **Sensitivity Reading Services:** Websites like https://sensitivityreviews.com/ offer curated lists of freelance sensitivity readers with expertise in various areas, including disabilities.
- **Social Media:** Similar to finding consultants, Twitter can be a useful tool to connect with sensitivity readers. Utilize relevant hashtags (#SensitivityReader, #DisabilitySensitivityReader) to find them.

Important Considerations:

- **Credentials:** Evaluate the consultant's or reader's experience and expertise in the specific SHALD you're portraying.
- **Disclosure:** Be upfront about your needs and the type of feedback you're seeking.

- **Compensation:** Disability consultants and sensitivity readers typically charge fees for their services. Be prepared to offer fair compensation for their time and expertise.

Additional Tips:

- Consider joining online communities for individuals with the specific SHALD you're depicting.
- Look for memoirs or autobiographies written by people with SHALDs to gain firsthand perspectives.

By collaborating with disability consultants and sensitivity readers, you gain valuable insights and ensure your portrayal of characters with SHALDs is respectful, authentic, and avoids perpetuating stereotypes.

Remember: The goal isn't to create a character defined solely by their SHALD. Instead, weave their communication differences into the rich tapestry of their personality. By portraying characters with SHALDs with empathy, authenticity, and respect, you can challenge stereotypes, promote inclusivity, and inspire understanding in your readers.

Breathing Life into Your Characters: Weaving Authenticity in Speech, Hearing & Language Disorders

Speech, hearing, and language disorders (SHALDs) shape how characters interact with the world. By incorporating these nuances, you can craft characters with SHALDs who feel genuine and relatable. Here's how to infuse authenticity:

Dialogue and Interaction: A Tapestry of Communication

- **Speech Patterns:** Research how the specific SHALD affects speech patterns. This might involve incorporating substitutions, repetitions, or hesitations for a stutter, or simpler sentence structures for aphasia.
- **Communication Challenges:** Don't shy away from realistic struggles. Show characters using assistive devices, asking for clarification, or experiencing frustration during conversations.

Balancing Authenticity with Clarity

- **Maintaining Narrative Flow:** Strive for authenticity, but ensure the dialogue remains understandable for readers. Use internal monologues or narration to explain communication breakdowns without compromising the story's flow.

Internal Monologue: A Window into the Soul

- **Inner Struggles:** Explore the character's internal world through internal monologues. Delve into their anxieties about communication breakdowns, frustrations with being misunderstood, or triumphs in overcoming challenges.

Perspectives on SHALDs

- **Acceptance and Denial:** SHALDs can evoke a range of emotions. Show characters grappling with acceptance, denial, or even anger towards their disorder.
- **Emotional and Cognitive Complexity:** Go beyond frustration. Explore the impact on self-confidence, social anxiety, or even depression. Consider how the disorder affects their thoughts and cognitive processes.

Remember:

Authenticity doesn't mean replicating every detail. It's about capturing the essence of the communication challenges and their emotional impact. By weaving these elements into dialogue, internal monologues, and character development, you create a portrayal that's both true to life and deeply engaging for your readers.

Bonus Tip: Consider including sensory details! How does the world sound different for someone with hearing loss? How might someone with apraxia of speech struggle to describe a beautiful sunset? Sensory details can add depth and authenticity to your portrayal.

Please note:

The information presented in this book is intended to provide writers with a general understanding of communication disorders. It is not a replacement for a professional evaluation by a qualified Speech–Language Pathologist (SLP). If you suspect someone may have a communication disorder, please consult with an SLP for diagnosis and treatment recommendations.

13

Conclusion

Farewell, But the Story Continues: Celebrating the Symphony of Everyday Communication

As we close the curtain on our exploration of Speech, Hearing, and Language Disorders (SHALDs) in literature, a chorus of voices rises in our hearts. This journey wasn't just about creating characters; it was about crafting a richer symphony of human experience, where every voice plays a unique and important part. We've delved into the complexities of communication, and how stories can foster empathy and understanding for the diverse ways we connect.

The Ripple Effect: Everyday Inspiration

Literature has the power to dismantle stereotypes and raise awareness in a way that clinical descriptions can't. By including characters with SHALDs in your narratives, you're not just telling a story – you're giving a voice to real experiences. Readers gain a deeper understanding of the challenges and triumphs faced by individuals with SHALDs, moving beyond medical terms to the vibrant tapestry of everyday life.

A New Chapter Begins: Reflecting the Everyday

This isn't the end of the story, but a new chapter filled with possibilities. As you embark on your writing journey, remember that characters with SHALDs come in all shapes, sizes, and voices. Just like describing a character's hair color or body type, consider including communication differences as a natural part of who they are.

Think Beyond the Spotlight: Incorporating Everyday Challenges

It's easy to be drawn to dramatic portrayals, but the reality of SHALDs is often more nuanced. Many people navigate communication challenges that might seem minor at first glance – a slight stutter that trips them up in social situations, difficulty finding the right word in a conversation, or needing a little extra time to process information during meetings.

Remember:

These "everyday" challenges can have a significant impact on a person's life. Just like the characters with more obvious SHALDs, they too deserve to be seen, heard, and celebrated in your stories. By reflecting this spectrum of experiences, you create a more inclusive and relatable world for your readers.

Continuing the Conversation: Resources for Your Journey

To deepen your understanding and keep the conversation flowing, here are some resources to explore: (*See also* **For More Information** *sections included in each chapter*)

Please note:

The information presented in this book is intended to provide writers with a general understanding of communication disorders. It is not a replacement for a professional evaluation by a qualified Speech-Language Pathologist (SLP). If you suspect someone may have a communication disorder, please consult with an SLP for diagnosis and treatment recommendations.

Resources for Researching Speech, Language, and Hearing Disorders

Books:

- **Stutterer** by Benjamin Pratt
- **Wonder** by R.J. Palacio (depicts a character with facial differences, but offers valuable insights into navigating social interactions when perceived as "different")
- **Silence is a Sentence** by Susie Knuckles (memoir by a woman with apraxia of speech)

Articles:

- **Research article (includes a rating form for disorder portrayal in children's literature):** Lefevre, Jane, *"The Portrayal of Protagonists with Communication Disorders in Contemporary Award-Winning Juvenile Fiction"* (2015). Graduate Theses, Dissertations, and Problem Reports. 6054. https://researchrepository.wvu.edu/etd/6054
- **12 Fascinating Stories about Adult Communication Disorders:** https://tactustherapy.com/stroke-stories-books-movies/
- **Annotated Bibliography Books and movies about communication impairments:** https://cdn.csu.edu.au/__data/assets/pdf_file/0005/3792398/Books-and-moviesaboutcommunicationimpairments.pdf

Films:

- **The King's Speech** (depicts King George VI's journey overcoming a stammer)
- **Coda** (features a character navigating the world as the only hearing member of a deaf family)
- **Temple Grandin** (features a character who has autism and was nonverbal into childhood)
- **Resources for Inclusion and Diversity in Special Education (IRIS):** https://iris.peabody.vanderbilt.edu/resources/films/
- **The Doctor** (features a character with a voice disorder secondary to laryngeal cancer)
- **My Left Foot** (main character has cerebral palsy and communicates by device using his left foot)
- **A Quiet Place 2** (main character is deaf with a cochlear implant)
- **The Diving Bell and the Butterfly** (Main character is a person completely paralyzed by a stroke, except for his left eye, who goes on to be journalist and editor of French Elle magazine)
- **Rocket Science** (main character who stutters and chooses to be true to himself)
- **The Farewell (2019):** This dramedy features a character, Nai Nai, who has a swallowing disorder. The film subtly shows the challenges she faces with eating and the adjustments her family makes to accommodate her needs.
- **Still Alice (2014):** This film follows Alice Howland's journey with early-onset Alzheimer's disease. As the disease progresses, she experiences difficulty swallowing.

Lectures and Public Announcements

- **My Stroke of Insight:** https://www.ted.com/talks/jill_bolte_taylor_my_stroke_of_insight

Organizations:

- **The National Stuttering Association:** National Stuttering Association stutteringhelp.org
- **The Alexander Graham Bell Association for the Deaf and Hard of Hearing:** Alexander Graham Bell Association for the Deaf and Hard of Hearing agbell.org
- **The American Speech-Language Hearing Association (ASHA):** asha.org/public/
- **National Association for Hearing and Speech Action (an affiliate of ASHA):** https://identifythesigns.org/signs-of-speech-and-language-disorders/
- **National Aphasia Association:** aphasia.org
- **National Institute on Deafness and Other Communication Disorders:** National Institute on Deafness and Other Communication Disorders: https://www.nidcd.nih.gov/

Health Websites:

- **Mayo Clinic:** Diseases and Conditions Speech and language disorders: https://www.mayoclinic.org/departments-centers/division-speech-pathology/overview/ovc-20443698
- **MedlinePlus:** https://medlineplus.gov/speechandcommunicationdisorders.html

The Power Lies in the Ordinary: Celebrating the Symphony of Communication

Ultimately, the power of literature lies in its ability to connect us with experiences beyond our own. By weaving characters with SHALDs into the fabric of your stories, you celebrate the beauty of communication in all its forms. Let your characters be the voice for those who are often unheard, and showcase the resilience of the human spirit in navigating the complexities of everyday communication.

This concludes our exploration, but the story doesn't end here. Let your characters be the heroes of their own narratives, celebrating the vibrant symphony of human communication.

Jennifer Tillock, M.S. CCC–SLP

DISCLAIMER

This book is intended for informational purposes only and is not a substitute for professional medical advice, diagnosis, or treatment. If you have any questions or concerns about a communication disorder, please consult a qualified Speech–Language Pathologist (SLP) or other medical professional.

About the Author

Jennifer Tillock is a speech-language pathologist (SLP) with over 24 years of experience working with children via teletherapy. Her passion lies in helping young people overcome communication challenges and reach their full potential.

Jennifer's dedication extends beyond the clinical setting. She is also the author of engaging children's communication books, designed to make therapy sessions fun and interactive.

When she's not empowering young minds, Jennifer enjoys her time as a writer under the pen name Christine Tellach, crafting captivating stories that blend genres like paranormal westerns and urban fantasy.

Jennifer embraces a life that balances tranquility and creativity. She resides in a rural setting, surrounded by nature, and finds inspiration from her spirited daughters, her devoted husband, and their zen farm dog.

As a lifelong learner and avid reader, Jennifer is constantly seeking new ways to improve her practice and inspire her readers.

You can connect with me on:

- https://christinetellach.blogspot.com
- https://www.facebook.com/profile.php?id=61558204403047
- https://www.instagram.com/christinetellach
- https://www.goodreads.com/author/show/49319048.Christine_Tellach

Also by Jennifer Tillock, M.S. CCC-SLP

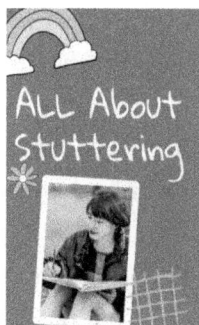

All About Stuttering

"All About Stuttering" is a fun, fact-filled adventure for kids who want to understand stuttering. This friendly guide explores the reasons why people stutter, the different ways it can sound, and most importantly, how to be a great friend to someone who stutters. With cool illustrations and clear explanations, kids will learn everything they need to know to celebrate the unique voices of all their friends!

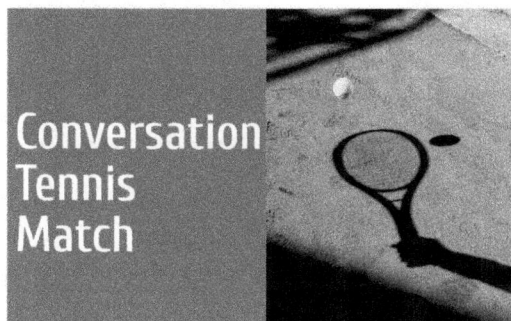

Conversation Tennis Match: A Social Story

Introducing **Conversation Tennis Match**, a social story designed to help kids learn about conversations in a fun and engaging way. We use the analogy of a tennis match to explain how conversations work. Just like in tennis, participants take turns "hitting" the conversation back and forth, ensuring that everyone has a chance to contribute. By comparing conversations to a tennis match, children can grasp the concept of turn-taking and mutual exchange more easily. The analogy makes abstract ideas more concrete and relatable. Includes ideas for additional activities in the classroom.

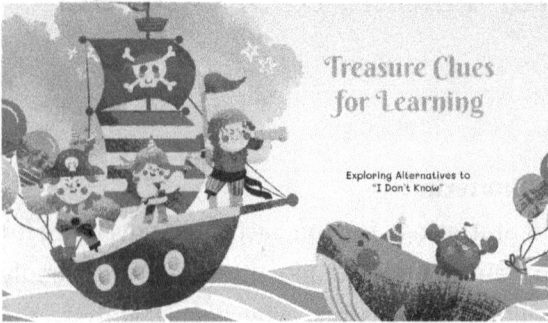

Treasure Clues for Learning: Exploring Alternatives to "I Don't Know"

Ditch "I Don't Know!" Set Sail for Learning Adventures!

Tired of the dreaded "I don't know" echoing in your classroom? Treasure Clues for Learning is your map to transform your classroom into a learning wonderland!

This book equips you with 12 powerful alternatives to "I don't know," empowering students to tackle challenges and become fearless explorers of knowledge.

But it's not just about the answers! You'll also learn why these alternatives are crucial for student growth and how to use them to guide your crew to success!

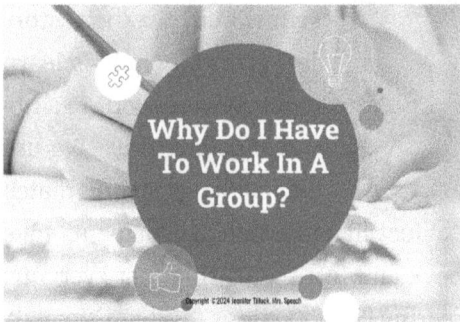

Why Do I Have To Work In A Group?

"Why Do I Have to Work In a Group?" addresses a common student complaint head-on. This book not only outlines the benefits of group work but also offers practical tips for successful collaboration. From enhancing teamwork skills to fostering creativity, this resource equips students with the tools they need to excel in group settings. Engage your students and transform their attitudes toward group projects with this invaluable resource!

The Wolves

Kidnapped by wolves. Awakened as an Alpha. Maya's camping trip takes a terrifying turn when she's snatched by a werewolf pack. Little does she know, she's one of them. Thrust into a hidden world of fangs and fur, Maya must master her newfound wolf form and navigate a web of danger.

There's Jack, her gruff captor-turned-protector. A growing pack to call family. And looming on the horizon, a deadly vampire threat. Can Maya embrace her destiny as Alpha and forge her place in this supernatural society? Or will she be torn between her human life and the power surging within?

Dive into this thrilling tale of transformation, love, and fierce loyalty. Where will Maya's howl lead her?

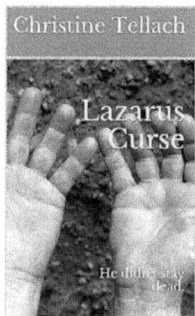

Lazarus Curse: He didn't stay dead
Buried Secrets. Uncertain Redemption.

Eli Colton walks a straight line in a small Texas town, a stark contrast to his outlaw past as Will Carter. Resurrected from the dead, he's offered escape from a life of violence, but the ghosts of his deeds linger. Eli craves redemption, a pursuit complicated by the internal demons he battles every day.

With his devoted dog Feather, Eli faces a constant struggle. Can he outrun the darkness that clings to him, or will his past drag him under? This thrilling Western paranormal tale explores love, sacrifice, and the relentless fight between a shadowed history and the desperate hope for a brighter future.

Will Eli find redemption, or will his buried secrets rise from the grave? Saddle up for a haunting adventure.

www.ingramcontent.com/pod-product-compliance
Lightning Source LLC
Chambersburg PA
CBHW070057030426
42335CB00016B/1925